Y0-BVO-636

This book is sponsored by the
Association of Evangelicals of Africa and Madagascar

OUR TIME HAS COME

The views expressed by the contributors to this book do not represent the official position of the Pan African Christian Women Assembly or of its parent body, the Association of Evangelicals of Africa and Madagascar.

OUR TIME HAS COME

edited by

JUDY MBUGUA

A15047 314651

Published on behalf of the
World Evangelical Fellowship by

BAKER BOOK HOUSE
Grand Rapids, Michigan

THE PATERNOSTER PRESS
Carlisle UK

British Library Cataloguing in Publication Data

Our Time Has Come
I. Mbugua, Judy W.
267.4096

ISBN 0–85364–525–6

Typeset by Photoprint, Torquay, Devon
and printed by
The Guernsey Press Co. Ltd., Guernsey, Channel Islands
for the publishers.

Contents

Preface

Your Excellency, the President and Head of State of the Republic of Kenya, the Ministers of Religion; Honourable Ministers and Members of the Parliament, Your Excellencies, the Ambassadors and Members of the Diplomatic Corps; Eminent Dignitaries; the Press; Friends and Well-wishers from near and far; Sisters and Brothers in the Lord; Ladies and Gentlemen; Greetings!

We count it as a great privilege and honour to have all of you present at this official opening of the first ever Pan African Christian Women Assembly (PACWA). In particular, we are humbled by your kindness, Your Excellency, in accepting our invitation to open this historic event which is destined to become a movement. This is further proof of your commitment to improve the dignity of women in our Continent.

Indeed PACWA is historic. It will be recalled that a couple of centuries ago our continent Africa was called a dark continent by her explorers. Her coasts were hazardous; her forests were impregnable; her pests were deadly; and her people savages. Many were those foreigners including missionaries who died and were buried on her soil. At the same time, Africa suffered from the hands of those who brutalized her people and raped her economic resources.

Today, the picture is different. All of Africa is free from foreign political domination. While her economy is still fledgling and her foreign debts soar (and pray for her redemption), the fact remains that Africa's destiny is in the hands of her people. In the international community of nations such as the United Nations, African nations can no longer be ignored. Beyond this, and for our immediate purpose, from Cairo in the north to Cape Town in the south; from Dakar in the west to Djibouti in the east, Jesus Christ is being recognized, embraced and worshipped as Lord! Indeed 'Ethiopia', which symbolically stands for Africa in biblical prophecy has suddenly stretched her hands unto God (Ps. 68:31).

While Africa may yet have other problems – and Your Excellency once described her as a bleeding continent – it can no longer be called a 'dark continent'. We are grateful to God and to those who brought the gospel to us. Therefore, this is a great day, an important day, a day to remember. Indeed it is the day that the Lord has made, and we will rejoice and be glad in him. It is a day for which we are grateful to God, for this Assembly PACWA has become a reality! We call it unique because it is the first of its kind in the last 100 years of Church history in Africa.

Your Excellency Sir, we command you for your able, competent dedicated and loving leadership both at home and throughout the continent of Africa. We also assure you of our continued prayers. What is PACWA and what do women mean when they boldly annouce 'Our time Has Come'? Does that mean they are no longer going to cook? This and many others may be some of the questions going on in many minds. Let me start by explaining what PACWA is. It stands for Pan African Christian Women Assembly. It is a movement that will start with an event – indeed this Assembly. The purpose of this movement is to bring together leading evangelical Christian women from the whole continent of Africa, so as to examine national, continental and world-wide issues that we encounter in our lives as women. Such issues for instance include AIDS, witchcraft, polygamy, the plight of the widow and her children, poverty and hunger, evangelism, sex abuse, social injustices and battered women, just to mention a few.

The result of the launching of this historical PACWA movement should mean the establishment of a necessary common front on various issues in order to chart a future course. Participants will be encouraged when they return to their homes to mobilize other women to offer a godly alternative in the struggle to alleviate the plight of women. They will be expected to play active and positive roles that can help to transform the world.

The time has come, therefore, for committed Christian women in Africa to unite our efforts to reach the nations of Africa for our Lord Jesus Christ. PACWA has one vision – to reach Africa for Jesus. So it is not time to compete with men but for us to complement each other.

Your Excellency Sir, PACWA is calling both men and women in church and society to recognize that the calling and mission of Christ is extended to the total family of God.

Therefore, the theme 'our time has come' should not threaten anybody. It firstly challenges women to rise up to the call of God in Luke 23:28 'But Jesus turning to them said, "Daughters of Jerusalem, do not weep for me, but weep for yourselves and for your children." ' Women cry for your children. Did you ever realize that each person here is the child of a mother? If all mothers cry for their children, God will hear and hold back his wrath from our generation. It is also a challenge to Christians to lessen the tension between sexes, to loosen chains that have bound women in the area of ministry and simply to recognize their potential. Working together in harmony will bring glory to God. But it is also time for men to realize that we are God's latest model of creation – the model with least problems. So we are asking men to give us a chance, an opportunity to use our God-given abilities.

Your Excellency Sir, the idea of this PACWA Assembly was first mentioned in Lusaka, Zambia, during the 5th General Assembly of the Association of Evangelicals in Africa and Madagascar (AEAM) in September 1987. In the interim, five Pre-PACWA mini-conferences have taken place. Two were in West Africa, in Burkina Faso for francophone and Ghana for anglophone Africa. Another took place in Zaire for Central Africa franco-phone, the one for the Southern region was held in Zimbabwe and the one for the East African region was held here in Nairobi. At each of the Pre-PACWA conferences, an average of 80 key Christian women attended and discussed pertinent issues affecting the Christian women in their region and in Africa as a whole. Various resolutions were passed. These resolutions include the following:

1. Whereas alcoholism has caused tremendous suffering in our homes and families, as PACWA women, we condemn the drinking of alcoholic beverages because of the serious consequences. We recommend that our churches address the issues of alcoholism through such activities as family counselling, retreats, Bible studies, youth conferences etc. in order to counteract the pressure that leads to drinking.
   We further recommend that alcoholics and their families be encouraged to seek medical help from institutions such as A.A, S.D.A., or hospitals.
2. As PACWA women, we encourage, support and stand by the view that monogamy is God's original intention for marriage and that polygamy is man's design not God's design and therefore, we recommend that the church should take a firm stand against polygamy because it is against the teaching of the Bible.
3. We recommend that the subject of bereavement be addressed in our churches and biblical principles be taught on it. We further recommend that the spiritual implications of cultural practices be dealt with in a Christ-like manner. We recommend that the government takes a serious look at the treatment traditionally meted out to widows with a view to legislating against some of the practices which dehumanize and undermine the Christian view of human dignity.
4. Whereas in the past the tendency of society has been to limit women to the roles of wife and mother, we recommend a change in approach which will give women equal opportunities to develop their educational abilities and talents to the maximum.
5. With the introduction in some primary schools of sex education (family planning), (higher grades), we recommend that parents be given the opportunity to listen to what their children are being taught and also to express their own views on such teaching.
6. Note has been taken of the government policy in some countries to provide opportunities for male prisoners to develop skills. Regrettably this privilege is denied to the female prisoners. We therefore urge governments to take urgent steps to equip female prisoners with relevant skills.
7. In the face of urbanization and eroding economies, we recommend that we commit ourselves to social concerns and social actions in various societies e.g. equipping prostitutes with skills which will enable them to fend for themselves, rehabilitating freed female prisoners, establishing day care centres for children staying with their mothers in prison.

These resolutions will form the PACWA mandate.

Your Excellency Sir, today the idea of the PACWA assembly is becoming reality. This PACWA movement will then be expected to inject biblical morals and values into the society of our beloved continent of Africa. Evangelical women have realized the need to make women recognize that they too have potential for greater effectiveness in both the Church and society. Women like Deborah and Esther have left their mark on history. Deborah was wife, prophetess, judge, warrior and singer. When Barak refused to go to war, in words which I quote from the Bible in Judges 4:6, 'The Lord, the God of Israel, commands you to go . . . into battle. Barak said – "No! Unless you go with me I will not go, but if you go with me I will go." Deborah said "I will go, but the honour will go to a woman!" ' In Africa there is the cry of corruption, hunger, and poverty. We can fight these evils only by obeying the Word of God. We are saying that we will go all the way with God.

Your Excellency, Sir, PACWA as a movement plans to have:

1. An equal level of education throughout the five regions of Africa.
2. A continental networking to bridge the regions.
3. National on-going workshops and seminars.
4. Massive production of diagnostic and educational tools. All these can be described as 'Christian Women Education by Extension'.

Your Excellency Sir, we have a strong conviction of the need for PACWA. It has taken great strides of faith financially. The whole PACWA programme was initiated in faith and has progressed in faith. But when the time comes for God to act, he always has a Mordecai ready. When it was time for Esther to save the Jews, God had prepared her uncle Mordecai who addressed her thus: 'If you remain silent at this time, relief and deliverance for the Jews will arise from another place, but you and your father's family will perish. And who knows but that you have come to the kingdom for such a time as this!' Who knows indeed? AEAM, like Mordecai of old have done their part. It has cost four million Kenya shillings to hold this Assembly and the Association of Evangelicals of Africa and Madagascar under the able leadership of their General Secretary Dr. Tokunboh Adeyemo have raised the funds. At this juncture, I wish, on behalf of the Executive Committee, to express PACWA's gratitude to AEAM for sponsoring this conference. Dr. Adeyemo, please thank all the donors on our behalf.

Your Excellency, there are many things we would like to ask of you and all those present. But like Solomon, we want to ask in wisdom. We ask for recognition and partnership. We will be coming to you to ask for the use of existing ministries and instruments to promote this movement to its highest potential. We ask that women be included and involved in the highest levels of decisions that affect women. We ask that PACWA be involved as a resource centre for issues that affect families. Your Excellency Sir, you will agree that women are the majority Kanu members, church attenders, teachers but have the fewest places in high-level decision-making bodies. Please include us.

Your Excellency Sir, this may look like an unnecessary appeal on behalf of women, but I have already said that women are God's latest model of creation. Not only that but they are made from better material! Men are made from mere dust, but women from ribs!

With these very few words, I would like to take this opportunity to invite Pastor Dennish White who will call on His Excellency to address this gathering and officially open this conference.

Introduction

J. W. MBUGUA

For the first time in the history of the church in Africa, a Pan African Christian Women Assembly (PACWA) got underway in Nairobi, Kenya, lasting for 7 days (6th August – 12th August 1989). This historic event sponsored by the Association of Evangelicals of Africa and Madagascar (AEAM) was two years in the making before its birth.

It began in September 1987 when the vision was communicated to the group of women attending the 5th General Assembly of the AEAM at Lusaka, Zambia. A Nairobi-based Committee kept the vision alive with fasting and prayers and hundreds of hours of strategic planning. This resulted in phasing PACWA into three:

1. Five regional pre-PACWA consultations
2. Main PACWA
3. PACWA follow-up

It was felt from the very beginning that PACWA was destined to become a movement. Lofty objectives were set up for PACWA, namely:

1. Carrying the gospel light to our people who are yet to be reached.
2. Stopping the tide of ungodly secularism and materialism.
3. Asserting the true dignity of women as found in God's Word.
4. Injecting into African society biblical morals and values through women who are the mothers of all societies.
5. Educating women on matters of justice, equity and socio-economic development.
6. Delivering Africa from moral decadence and ultimate collapse.
7. Fostering effective co-operation between all Christian women ministries in Africa.

The theme of the Conference, 'Our Time Has Come', seemed to stir all the women participants, including those who were reached through the mass media, especially during the grand official opening by the State President His Excellency Daniel Arap Moi (which received live coverage through the radio network). Christian women in the country warmed up to the launching of PACWA as they felt that finally they have one voice that can be heard in the highest place of authority in each nation.

The participants came from 36 African Nations including Namibia and South Africa. There were over 1650 participants who registered and an overflow of over 500 who did not register. They covered all walks of life: legal profession, politics, civil service, business, medical, ordained ministers of the Gospel, housewives, social workers, lecturers etc.

They spread over all the broad spectrum of Protestant Christianity: Anglican; Presbyterian; Lutheran; Methodist; Baptist; Pentecostal; Evangelical Free; and Charismatic. They shared many things in common:

1. their African womanhood
2. their concern for the plight of the African woman
3. their burden for Christian families
4. their passion for souls
5. their commitment to biblical righteousness and justice.

They were strongly *persuaded* that '. . . *righteousness exalts a nation . . .*' and that if Africa's many problems were to be solved, then she had better turn to God. They *also believed* they could be used of God as a solution.

It was recalled that a couple of centuries ago, Africa was called a dark continent by her explorers. Her coasts were hazardous; her forests were impregnable; her pests were deadly, and her people savages. Many were those foreigners including missionaries who died and were buried on her soil. Similarly, Africa suffered from the hand of those who brutalized her people and raped her economic resources.

Today this picture has changed. All of Africa is free from foreign political domination. Though her economy is still fledgling and her foreign debts soaring (we pray for her redemption), the fact remains that Africa's destiny is in the hands of her people.

In the International Community of Nations such as the United Nations, African nations can no longer be ignored. For our immediate purpose, from Cairo in the North to Cape Town in the South, from Dakar in the West to Djibouti in the East, Jesus Christ is being recognized, embraced and worshipped as Lord.

Indeed, 'Ethiopia', which symbolically stands for Africa in biblical prophecy has suddenly stretched her hands unto God (Psalm 68:3).

While Africa may yet have other problems, it can no longer be called a 'dark continent'; it may be a 'bleeding continent'. We are grateful to God and to those who brought the gospel to us. From where they left off, PACWA is determined to complete the task.

PACWA establishes a common front to tackle issues such as AIDS, witchcraft, polygamy, that of the widow's plight and her children, poverty, hunger, sex abuse, social injustices and discipleship evangelism.

The time has come for committed Christian women in Africa to unite efforts to reach our nations for the Lord Jesus Christ. Our vision is one: to reach Africa for Jesus. This does not mean we are competing with men, but we are complementing them.

The theme 'Our Time Has Come' was provocative and challenging. It calls on women to take seriously the message of Luke 23:28 'But Jesus turning to them said, "Daughters of Jerusalem, do not weep for me; but weep for yourselves and for your children" '.

Each person is born of a mother; if all mothers cry for their children, God will hear and turn away his wrath against our generation.

It is also a challenge to Christians to lessen the tension between sexes, to loosen the chains that have been put around women regarding ministry and to simply recognize the potential they have. Thereafter the glorious fruits of working together in harmony will bring glory to God.

Prior to this historic assembly, there were 5 Pre-PACWA conferences:

Two in West Africa – for Francophone in Burkina Faso and for Anglophone in Ghana.

One in Central Africa Francophone – in Zaire.

One in Southern Africa Anglophone – in Zimbabwe.

One in Eastern Africa Anglophone – in Kenya.

The average attendance was 80 key Christian women, to discuss pertinent issues affecting the Christian women in their respective regions and in Africa as a whole. Some of the resolutions passed in the Pre-PACWA (in summary) are:

1. Alcoholism – the women condemned alcoholism which has caused great suffering to various families.
2. Polygamy – the women's stand is that God's design for marriage was monogamy.
3. Sex Education – women should have a chance to know what their children are being taught in schools.
4. Widowhood – the women desire to be protected against cultural practices that do not have Christian dignity.
5. Opportunities – the women desire to have equal opportunities available for both men and women.
6. Female prisoners – female prisoners should be equipped with relevant skills to assist them to earn a living when free.
7. Urbanization and Eroded Economy – social concern and action.

A women's desk has been set up under the AEAM as a Commission on Women Affairs to follow up the resolutions agreed upon during Pre-PACWA activities. The PACWA programme is designed to run in five tracks, a pattern of what is to become the five-fold ministry of PACWA.

POST PACWA TRACK CONCENTRATIONS

1. Networking all the Existing Women Ministry Models in Africa:

Practitioners came from all over Africa to tell the stories of their ministries and share their various experiences. Iron indeed sharpens iron. A directory is available, of this subject matter.

2. Social-Economic and Cultural Issues Plaguing African Women:

Under this, polygamy, battered women, AIDS, abortions, social injustice, sexual abuse and the role of women in society were tackled. Most of the

papers are available in the following pages. Research continues in the
PACWA office.

3. Women Empowerment:

Different ways by which women in difficulties could be helped out of their
situation of powerlessness were considered. The approaches examined
included: self-help projects; co-operatives; small scale industries and setting
up professional assistance such as legal advice and counselling ministry.

4. Spiritual Enrichment:

For women in particular and Christian homes in general. Emphasis was
placed on Bible Study, Prayer, Character Formation, Commitment to Christ,
Spiritual Gifts, Stewardship and being a Woman of God. *Resource Teams* are
organized to carry on this ministry throughout Africa.

5. The Great Commission:

Various forms of Evangelism currently employed by women including Child
Evangelism; Literacy and Evangelism; Prison Ministry and Hospital Visitation were re-appraised for better future effectiveness.

The PACWA Movement shall be expected to steer its assigned duties as it
injects biblical morals and values into our beloved continent. Taking an
example from biblical women like Deborah and Esther, the Evangelical
women see an urgent need to take action. Deborah, for instance, was a wife,
prophetess, judge, warrior and singer. When Barak refused to go to war
(Judges 4:6), Deborah went with him and the honour had to go to a woman.
In Africa, there is a cry against corruption, hunger and poverty. We can fight
these evils only by obeying the Word of God. We are saying that we will go all
the way with God using these channels:

a) Grass-root level education process throughout the seven regions (for
   PACWA purposes, Africa is now divided into seven regions).
b) Continental networking to bridge the regions.
c) National on-going workshops.
d) Mass production of diagnostic educational tools.

In total, the above can be described as 'Christian Women Education by
Extension'.

PACWA has taken great strides of faith financially. The programme was
initiated by faith and through the use of his servants like Mordecai of the Old
Testament, God used the General Secretary of the Association of Evangelicals of Africa and Madagascar, Dr. Tokunboh Adeyemo, to see PACWA
become a reality. PACWA therefore requests recognition and partnership
from all the governments of Africa so that it can attain its highest potential as
stipulated in the PACWA Covenant and PACWA Resolutions.

Part One

Our Time Has Come:
The Woman God Uses

1

A Woman of Excellence
(Ruth 3:10–11)
Keynote Address for PACWA Phase II

TOKUNBOH ADEYEMO

By the grace of God the first ever Pan African Christian Women's Assembly is taking place this week at Nairobi. It has been a long time coming. In spite of numerous forms of opposition, barriers and difficulties, God has brought you safely from all over Africa (and beyond) to celebrate, worship, work and witness the birth of PACWA, a Christian women's movement that is destined to have a far reaching impact upon Africa. Your being here is not by accident, but by divine appointment. To God, who has made PACWA possible and made you part of it be all the glory!

We salute the PACWA Executive Committee and International Council under the competent leadership of Judy Mbugua for their vision, stubborn faith, dedication to duty, earnest prayers and personal sacrifices. You have worked for a long time and over many hours in preparation for PACWA. We dearly appreciate your labour of love and commend you to the Lord for his rich benedictions.

On behalf of the Executive Committee and the entire family of AEAM throughout Africa, I welcome all of you to this phase of PACWA. It is my prayer that your time together might be blessed of the Lord by his presence and power in order that you might discover his purpose and do his will. I am grateful to the Committee for the honour of being asked to address you today. Since I was asked, the Lord has laid it upon my heart to address you on 'Being a Woman of Excellence'. The focus of our reflection is Ruth, and our text is Ruth 3:10–11:

> Then he said, 'May you be blessed of the Lord, my daughter. You have shown your last kindness to be better than the first by not going after young men, poor or rich. And now, my daughter, do not fear. I will do for you whatever you ask, for all my people in the city know that you are *a women of excellence*' (NASV).

DEFINITION OF TERMS

Excellence speaks of nobility; virtue; greatness; pre-eminence; surpassing merit. To be excellent is to be superior to others in character and in deeds. It is to be morally upright and prudent in judgement. Throughout the Scriptures, excellence is used in different contexts with reference to moral strength, mental ability, efficiency, wealth and valour. Excellence is a term that is used in reference to Kings, heads of States, ambassadors, and people of noble birth. An excellent score in a test signifies the best possible. Anything higher than that has to be qualified by 'more' or 'most'. Excellence brings to our minds something perfect, leaving room for little or no improvement.

As PACWA women, this is my prayer for you: that you may be all that God intends for you to be in Jesus Christ: 'all my people in the city know that you are a women of excellence'. In what ways did Ruth excel over other women around her? Briefly, we want to isolate four areas:

1. Her Faith in God
2. Her Industriousness
3. Her Fidelity (Loyalty) to people, and
4. Her Moral Purity

Her Faith in Yahweh

Ruth was a Gentile woman from Moab. As you may know, the Moabites are descendants of Lot. Following the destruction of Sodom and Gomorrah and the turning into a pillar of salt of Lot's wife, his two daughters despaired of any future. In faithless irresponsibility, they got their father drunk enough to go to bed with them. The fruit of that incest were Moab and Ben Ammi who become the ancestors of the Moabites and the Ammonites, nations that often warred against Israel. These nations drifted away from any knowledge of Yahweh that Lot might have had and became totally idolatrous. This was Ruth's background and upbringing.

But Ruth broke that tradition of idolatry. Through her marriage to Mahlon, a Hebrew from Bethlehem, she became a believer in Yahweh, the Living God of Israel. Faith for Ruth is coming to seek refuge under the wings of the Almighty (2:12). From this point on her life was characterized by complete trust in Jehovah. Her faith in God was so unshakeable that ten years of childlessness did not drive her back to the pagan practice of consulting a witch-doctor or a diviner. And when the worst came and her husband was taken by death, she remained unmoved. But someone may ask: 'In what way was Ruth's faith greater than Orpah's – Ruth's sister-in-law married to Chilion, Mahlon's brother who suffered the same calamity?' Our answer will be in its endurance. For it is only faith that endures to the end that God rewards.

You will recall that after Naomi, their embittered mother-in-law who had suffered the loss of her husband and two sons, told her two daughters-in-law to return to their mothers houses, Orpah went back. Why? Because in their culture (like ours), marriage meant security for a woman. Yet Ruth by faith was giving that up by leaving Moab. Ruth chose to follow her widowed mother-in-law even when this meant she would never have a husband or children. To the rational mind, Ruth's decision was foolish and irrational. But isn't this what faith means sometimes? God uses the foolish to confound the wise; and the weak to confound the strong. Naomi did not make it easy for Ruth to embrace faith in God either. But Ruth persevered and her faith endured. Listen to Naomi: 'Behold, your sister-in-law has gone back to her people and her gods; return after your sister-in-law.' Now listen to Ruth's response:

> Do not urge me to leave you or to turn back from following you: for where you go, I will go, and where you lodge, I will lodge. Your people shall be my people, and your God, my God. Where you die, there I will be buried. Thus may the Lord do to me, and worse, if anything but death parts you and me.

In all of the world's literature, this beautiful expression of faithful commitment by Ruth stands out. She made a complete break with the past to face an uncertain future. There were no signs in the sky, no dream, and no promise. The facts of her widow-hood and of her mother-in-law's discouragement challenged her decision to have faith in God. Indeed, 'Faith is the assurance of things hoped for, the conviction of things not seen' (Heb. 11:1). By faith Ruth chose a 'ridiculous' life with Naomi rather than her family, her nation, and her idolatrous religion. But in God's economy, this is the first step to excellence.

The writer of Hebrews says: 'By faith the men of old gained God's approval'; and 'without it, it is impossible to please God' (11:2, 6).

PACWA women, the challenges before you are enormous. You are up against giants and rightly feel like grasshoppers. But with faith in God you can meet these challenges. You can be God's instruments to right the wrongs of our rapidly detoriorating society. You can be used of God to stop families falling apart in our society. You can be salt and light in our world of injustices, discrimination and corruption. You can serve as 'balm of Gilead' to bring healing to our brokenness and hope to the hopeless. You can rise in obedience to Christ's Commission to finish the task of world evangelization. Yes, you can! At a time when men seem to be drifting and churches are getting cold, with your fervent prayers you can bring about spiritual revival! Yet not you; but God working in and through you. This is your first step to excellence: stubborn faith in God, the Father of our Lord Jesus Christ.

Her Industriousness

Ruth's second area of excellence was her industriousness. Diligent hard work; habitual useful employment both at home and out in the field marked the life of Ruth. Back in Bethlehem with Naomi, Ruth could have allowed her mother-in-law's bitterness to make her depressed and utterly discouraged. But as Sir Joshua Reynolds says: 'Excellence is never granted to man, but as the reward of labour. It argues, indeed, no small strength of mind to persevere in the habits of industry . . .' Some people believe that all we have to do is have faith in God. They are wrong. For the Bible says: 'We are his workmanship, created in Christ Jesus for good works . . .' (Eph. 2:10). Here we see that faith and works go hand-in-hand. While Naomi stayed home, perhaps because of old age, Ruth worked hard in the field gleaning the ears of grain after the harvesters. She was diligent. The record says that she gleaned in the field from the morning till the evening with a lunch break with Boaz in-between (2:7, 14–17).

A theology of work is desperately needed today, especially in our cities. Many young people rush to the cities looking for 'white collar jobs'. When hopes are dashed many have turned to prostitution, stealing and subversive activities. The church needs to restore the dignity of work.

Paul writes: 'If anyone does not work, he shouldn't eat'. In another place he says: 'If anyone does not provide for his own . . . he has denied the faith, and is worse than an unbeliever. Let a widow be put on the welfare list only if she is not less than sixty years old, having been the wife of one man, having a reputation for good works; and if she has brought up children, if she has shown hospitality to strangers, if she has washed the saints feet, if she has assisted those in distress, and if she has devoted herself to every good work' (1 Tim. 5:8–10).

African women have a legacy of hard work. Whether at home or in the fields (shamba); whether in business or in professions; whether in social works or in philanthropy; in the chambers of commerce as well as the courts of law; in war time as well as in peace time, your record of diligent work is above reproach. Many are the mothers who have worked single-handedly to put their children through school. Many still do. I salute all those Christian women who believe in and practise hard work. You must increase in this virtue. Study Proverb 31 and you will discover that you are in the list of God's excellent women. Where this tradition has broken down, African Christian women should help to redeem and restore it. Ruth combined her faith in Yahweh with diligent hard work. Just as walking requires two legs, these two virtues help her to progress towards excellence.

Her Fidelity (Loyalty; Faithfulness) to People

Ruth's third area of excellence was her faithful concern for people. Her concern for Naomi is classic. She followed her; clung to her; served her; went out to work and brought food home for her; confided in her; and obeyed her. In a world of strained relationships, broken homes and joyless marriages often caused by 'mothers-out-law', what a refreshing and shining example Ruth presents to us! She refused to abandon her mother-in-law. Her love for Naomi was as pure as gold and as strong as death. Many waters could not quench it. Her loyalty for Naomi was an example of the purest and most unselfish form of devotion. All the people in the city knew it. Listen to their comment following the birth of a son by Ruth to Boaz:

'May he also be to you a restorer of life, and a sustainer of your old age; for your daughter-in-law, who loves you and is better to you than seven sons, has given birth to him' (4:15). If this was said by the women, what do the men say?

Let Boaz speak for them. In 2:11 Boaz answered and said to her: 'All that you have done for your mother-in-law after the death of your husband has been fully reported to me, and how you left your father and your mother and the land of your birth, and came to a people that you did not previously know. May the Lord reward your work . . .'.

As you work through the issues before you this week, you will discover that issues ultimately have to do with people. Whether they concern AIDS or abortion; child abuse or social injustices; evangelism or social concern; they will concern people. These people may be harrassed and helpless; in trouble and disgrace; in power or in poverty. Ultimately, issues are people. Tackle the issues with seriousness. But remember to deal with people with compassion. It was compassion that made Jesus:

- heal every sickness and disease (Mt. 14:14)
- feed the hungry multitudes (Mt. 15:32)
- restore sight to the blind (Mt. 20:34)
- cleanse the lepers (Mk. 1:41)
- raise the dead (Lk. 7:13)
- weep at the grave of Lazarus (Jn. 11:33, 35)

Yes, it was compassion that sent Mother Teresa to the slums of Calcutta. Like the good Samaritan, compassion may force you to pause in the course of this conference to ask: 'Lord, what can I do in order to change my world for Christ?' You may be weak and powerless as men say. But if you loved your nation as Esther did Israel, God may use you to bring deliverance to your people. Millions are still lost today without Christ and without hope. Only with love under the anointing of the Holy Spirit can we reach them.

The power of love in Ruth's story is breath-taking. It breaks down barriers. It unites Jew and Gentile; rich and poor (Boaz and Ruth); old and young (Naomi and Ruth); royalty and commoner. This is what the love of Christ does by the power of the gospel.

Her Moral Purity

The beauty and power of Ruth's moral purity can be seen only against the background of the irresponsible and sensual activities of the Judges. Many of them, like Gideon and Samson, were mighty in physical strength but weak in spiritual and moral character. Theirs was a time of sexual permissiveness. Polygamy and concubinage were common. It was during this period that the events of the book of Ruth took place (1:1). The repeated theme of the days of the Judges is that 'there was no king in Israel and everyone did what was right in his own eyes' (Judg. 21:25). Lawlessness, permissiveness and irresponsible living characterized the period.

In the midst of this, Ruth, a young widow kept herself pure. The poor, strangers and lonely widows often succumb to irresponsible and illicit sex. But this will not be so for godly Ruth. Her faith in God will sustain her; her industry will keep her dignity; and her moral strength will make her a heroine! She commanded respect from all. It is in this context that Boaz made his remarkable statement: 'You have shown your last kindness to be better than the first by not going after young men, whether poor or rich . . . for all my people in the city know that you are a woman of excellence' (3:10–11).

Another aspect of her moral strength can be seen in her compliance with the law of levirate marriage and the kinsman-redeemer provision in case of the death of a husband leaving no child behind. Ruth 4:9–17 discloses how Boaz, of the family of Elimelich, Ruth's father-in-law, fulfilled this obligation. In this regard, Ruth was more honourable than Tamar, who tricked Judah, her father-in-law into a love affair (Gen. 38:7–30). For Ruth, purity means no disguise and no seduction.

This path to excellence is hazardous and slippery. Many are the great men and women who have fallen back at this point. And at this point, the world is quick to judge the church. If I understand the Scriptures correctly, no other sin so rapidly diminshes a man or woman of God and removes glory from God as the sin of immorality. This is the way the apostle Paul understood it. He writes: 'Flee immorality. Every other sin that a man commits is outside his body, but the immoral man sins against his own body which is the temple of the Holy Spirit' (1 Cor. 6:18–20). It is so serious that Paul later says: 'I buffet my body and make it my slave, lest possibly, after I have preached to others, I myself should be disqualified' (1 Cor. 9:27).

As always, Ruth's moral chastity was greatly rewarded. Ten years of childless marriage – she waited! Then an unspecified period of widow-hood – she waited again. Finally, in his own time, the Lord brought her and Boaz together and enabled her to conceive, and she gave birth to a son, Obed, 'a servant who worships' (4:13, 17). By this marriage and the birth of Obed, Ruth became the great grandmother of David and an ancestor of our Lord Jesus Christ (Mt. 1:5). What honour can be greater than that? Her story is of a rise from rags to riches; from poverty to plenty; and from obscurity to prominence. Of the two books named after women in the Bible (Esther and Ruth), she was the first, and that, a Gentile!

CONCLUSION

As PACWA women what can we learn from this story?

- That faith in God can move a mountain.
- That industriousness restores human dignity.
- That compassion for people frees us.
- That moral purity elevates us.

Together – faith, industry, love and purity – these four ingredients will make you 'a woman of excellence'. As Ruth became immortalized, in Christ, you too can become immortalized.

2

Spiritual Leadership

REGINA AGBOZO

My task this morning is three-fold, to define:

1. What Spiritual Leadership is
2. What makes a Spiritual Leader
3. What qualities to look for in a Spiritual Leader

WHAT SPIRITUAL LEADERSHIP IS

Leadership is influence – one can lead others only to the extent that one can influence them. Leadership is the capacity to rally people to a common purpose, and the character which inspires confidence.

There is *natural* as well as *spiritual* leadership. Natural leadership can be conferred on a person by others, taken by force, or exerted by the sheer influence of a person's personality.

A spiritual leader, however, influences others not by the power of his own personality but by the extent to which he allows the Holy Spirit to control and flow through him to others. Spiritual leadership is conferred on a person *only* by God himself. This happens mostly to the most unlikely people, humanly speaking, or sometimes to the most reluctant. For while men look at the outward appearance, God looks at the heart.

A spiritual leader is likely to be a person who has no desire to lead, but who is put into a position of leadership by the inward pressure of the Holy Spirit and the pressure of external situations. All the great leaders in the Bible were people who were chosen by God and empowered by the Holy Spirit to fill positions which they felt unqualified to undertake by themselves – Moses, Gideon, Paul.

After the creation the fall thwarted God's intention for men and the need arose to call special men to provide leadership and to build God's kingdom (Gen. 1–15).

God raised prophets such as Moses and Samuel. He appointed judges such as Samson and Gideon. He chose priests such as Aaron, and he raised up kings like David.

Then in the fulness of time God sent forth his son (Gal. 4:4) to fulfil the promise given in Gen. 3:15.

Jesus Christ has through his death on the Cross and his resurrection restored man to the position of spiritual leadership which he lost in the Garden of Eden.

In Luke 9 and 10 Jesus Christ sent out the twelve, then the seventy disciples after giving them spiritual authority and power to subdue demons and to begin the building of his Kingdom (Luke 10:9–11).

In John 21:15–17, he singles out Peter after he has asked him three times whether Peter loved him and then commissioned him to feed his lambs and sheep, thus calling him to be a spiritual leader. Why Peter, one may ask? It was because it was Peter who said in Matthew 16:16, 'Thou art the Christ the Son of the living God.'

By implication therefore anyone who makes that confession has been given spiritual authority and thus leadership. That is why the Bible says in Matthew 5:13–14 that Christians are the salt and light of the world. Salt seasons a rotten society and light shows the way in darkness – that is spiritual leadership. However, many are called but few are chosen (Matt. 22:14).

WHAT MAKES A SPIRITUAL LEADER? – MOSES AND PETER

Though all Christians are supposed to be spiritual leaders, only a few meet God's criteria and are therefore chosen to lead. A person's ability to allow the Holy Spirit to flow through him so that he can influence men for good is that which makes him a spiritual leader.

Qualities to look for in a Spiritual Leader

Obviously one must be born again of the Spirit of God and filled with the Holy Ghost. Spiritual work is done in the Spirit not in the flesh (Ex. 2:11–15).

One must have heard the call of God and obeyed it.

One must be a person with a clear *vision* of what God wants one to do and a deep insight into prevailing situations and conditions (Prov. 29:18).

One must hold fast to sound biblical doctrine (2 Thes. 2:13–14. 1 Cor. 16:13). One must be steadfast. It is easy to change masters. Other qualities are also needed (Joshua 23:7–8. 1 Cor. 15:58).

Courage and Boldness The Holy Spirit gives boldness and courage to a spiritual leader to carry through the purposes of God – Peter before and after Pentecost is a classic example as is Moses before Pharaoh and Esther before the King.

Discipline To be a spiritual leader it is necesary first to submit to discipline and then to practise even greater self-discipline – discipline in hard work, in facing up to difficult situations, in deportment, in speech and even in eating. Moses learnt discipline at a very high cost – contrast Exodus 2:11–12 with Exodus 4:1; so did Peter (John 18:10 with John 18:17). God teaches his people discipline in the furnace of affliction, disgrace and failure with its resulting sense of unworthiness.

Wisdom and Tact   We need wisdom in handling explosive situations and difficult people. This was the wisdom King Solomon prayed for and received. It was shown by Abigail (1 Sam. 25:3, 18–33). In the church it is one of the gifts of the Holy Spirit.

Humility   One of the great dangers that can destroy a spiritual leader is *pride* especially when the Lord begins to use him. Great caution is needed here to emulate our Lord Jesus, who humbled himself and became obedient unto death. Jesus said: 'Take my yoke and learn of me for I am meek and lowly in heart and you shall find rest for your souls.'

A spiritual leader must consider himself a servant not a master – Paul says, 'I am the least of the apostles, I am the chief of sinners, I am less than the least of all the saints.' Be a servant of servants. The lower you go the higher the Lord will raise you up.

Faith   Faith in God will keep a spiritual leader undisturbed in the midst of disturbance. When the hounds of hell are let loose around you, faith in God will make you experience the truth that he that is in you is greater than all those without (Jn. 4:4). To listen to what God says and to cling to it when all around you are saying something else is a necessary requirement of a spiritual leader if he is to see the glory of his Lord, and his mission accomplished. Faith is the means through which the victory gained at Calvary over Satan and his hosts reaches the captives and delivers them. Hebrews 11 gives us both a definition and a catalogue of men and women of faith. 'Without faith it is impossible to please God' (Heb. 11:2).

Prayer and Fasting   Like his master, the spiritual leader must be a person of prayer and much fasting. More things are wrought by prayer than the world dreams of. Nehemiah, Queen Esther, Elijah, other prophets, the apostles, are examples of this. Prayer must not merely be an exercise for certain seasons, but an integral part of ordinary living and working. Prayer without ceasing is the command of the apostle Paul (1 Thes. 5:14). Moses often went to God in prayer and so did Peter. Remember his impetuous cry – 'Lord save me lest I perish!' Scripture is full of great things achieved for the glory of God through prayer and fasting. A spiritual leader must be far ahead of his followers in prayer and in fasting. According to Ephesians 6:18 prayer is part of our spiritual warfare. Our weapons are not carnal. Prayer is one of the greatest weapons the spiritual leader has in his fight against the principalities and powers he needs to contend with.

Patience   To lead others one must be able to master one's own temper and be calm in times of stress, to remain cool and unperturbed in times of severe criticism and be able to wait patiently to see the hand of the Lord move. 'If the vision tarries wait for it. It shall surely come' (Hab. 2:3). Patience is pressing on relentlessly when all visible signs are contrary to expectations. Patience is a beauiful fruit of the spirit. 'I waited patiently for the Lord and he inclined his ear unto me' (Ps. 40:1). Patience is planting and waiting for the harvest.

Order   A leader must be able to create a sense of order in all he does – he needs organizational ability and a sense of accountability not only to God but also to those he leads.

Suffering   Jesus gave the last drop of blood in his veins to redeem the world. His disciples are expected to do likewise. Whoever holds the first position among men must be everybody's slave.

There is a cost to be paid in leadership. Scars are authentic marks of spiritual leadership. Jesus' disciples did not recognize him nor his message on the road to Emmaus until he showed them his hands, the scars of his suffering. A disciple is never above his master. What they did to him they will do to you. Paul writes, 'From henceforth let no one trouble me for I bear in my body the marks of the Lord Jesus' (Gal. 6:17).

Self Sacrifice   A cross stands in the way of spiritual leaders, a cross which the leader must consent to bear. In John 3:16 we are told that Jesus laid down his life for us and we must lay down our life for the brethren. Suffering comes in varying forms and ways but it will always be there.

Hebrews 11 provides a catalogue of spiritual leaders, men and women who were called to service through sacrifice. God's plan does not change and will not change for anyone. The bitter cup must be drunk by all who are called to be spiritual leaders.

Suffering of all kinds is the main channel through which God prepares his soldiers for service. 'All who will live godly lives in Jesus will suffer persecution' (2 Tim. 3:12). A spiritual leader must therefore be prepared for suffering in various ways and forms.

Loneliness, rejection, fatigue, criticism, pressure and perplexity, temptations of all kinds come to spiritual leaders. (Above all a spiritual leader must meet the conditions stated by Paul in 1 Tim. 3:2–7 in his personal and domestic life.) The cost of leadership comes not only to the leader but to those around him, the children and the entire family. One must spend and be spent for Christ.

Love   Love must be the fundamental requirement of all spiritual leaders. Because they need to admonish and correct others, they must *not* harbour bitterness. They must be ready to show forgiveness.

These are the qualities to look for in a spiritual leader

Ability to train others
Ability to discipline in love
Ability to offer guidance
Initiative – the ability to initiate new ventures
Ability to undertake and accept responsibility
Knowledge of how to handle time and the people God gives him to work with
Ability to keep his tongue from speaking too much
Not to expect praise
Not to seek favour or pity
Not to be disturbed at unfairness to himself but to give thanks
Not to compromise in spiritual things

To be able to meet and master the jealousy of others
Ability to delegate responsibility and authority to others
Ability to appreciate the gifts of others and allow them to exercise such gifts in the Ministry
A concern for God's glory not one's own prestige.

3

Prayer and Spiritual Warfare

LOIS WAFULA

Luke 18:1 . . . 'That men ought always to pray and not faint'.

WHAT IS PRAYER?

'The potency of prayer has subdued the strength of fire, it has bridled the rage of lions, hushed storms to rest, extinguished wars, appeased the elements, expelled demons, burst the chains of death, expanded the gates of heaven, assuaged diseases, repelled frauds, preserved cities from destruction, stayed the sun in its course and arrested the progress of the thunderbolt. Prayer is an all-sufficient panoply, a treasure undiminished, a mine which is never exhausted, a sky unobscured by clouds, a heaven unruffled by storm. It is the root and the fountain of a thousand blessings.' Prayer in the cause of Christ is a conquering, and expanding force. It is talking to God on behalf of men.

It is the genius and mainspring of life. We live as we pray. The mercury of life rises only by the warmth of the prayer closet.

In the cause of Jesus Christ, prayer puts wings and power to the gospel so that it advances and conquers. Prayer is a condition of getting God's limitless aid. It is a channel through which all good flows from God to man and then from man to man. Prayer is the divinest engagement of man's reason. It is the wisest man who prays the most and the best. Prayer is real and vital work. In it lies the very heart of worship. Prayer is a solemn service due to God in adoration and worship. When we approach God with our requests our Father has the greatest pleasure in relieving the wants and granting the desires of his children. Again we see that prayer is the outstretched arms of the child for the father's help, the cry of the child to father's ear, and the father's heart.

Prayer is believing for specific things however great. Pray that they will come.

Prayer is the contact of a living soul with God. In prayer, God stops to kiss man, to bless man, and to help man in everything, filling man's emptiness with his own fulness.

It is poverty alleviated by God's riches.

It is weakness overcome by God's strength.

It is littleness banished by God's greatness.

It is a great continuous need met by God's continuous and abundant supply.

Prayer lifts men out earthliness and links them with the heavenlies.

Not to pray therefore is a crime in the moral spiritual government of God. It can bring only disorder and ruin.

'He knows not God, who knows not how to pray.' Prayerless lips reduce the gospel to dead orthodoxy.

Our best example is the Lord Jesus Christ's life of prayer which is summed up in Hebrews 5:7. 'Who in the days of his flesh when he had offered up prayers and supplication with strong crying and tears unto him that was able to save him from death and was HEARD in that he feared.'

WHY IS IT A WARFARE AND WHAT IS THE BATTLE ALL ABOUT?

Satan has suffered so much from the results of fervent praying that all his wily shrewed and ensaring devices are and will be used to cripple prayer.

Satan knows that God's promises will remain lying like corpses to fall into dust unless they are appropriated by earnest and prevailing prayer! Prayer provides and fertilizes the soil in which the promises of God can germinate. The purposes of God move to their glorious destinations along the pathway of prayer! The accuser of the brethren, the devil then dreads prayer. His work is to keep saints from prayer. This is his part of the war.

His Weapons

- Postponing prayer. We are too busy to pray. Our animals, people, and above all telephone calls will persistently interrupt prayer.
- A sense of worthlessness and despair. We think 'God can't listen to me. I am so tainted with sin, and the situation is really beyond help.'
- Doubts and impatience. Faith is the hand that receives from God. The wavering mind receives nothing from the Lord.
- Be patient: don't ring the bell and run. Wait for 'though it tarries it will surely come'. Elijah prayed seven times. The answer came!

WHAT IS OUR PART IN PRAYER?

First and foremost we must pray to save our nations from atheism, rationalism and scepticism through sound, quiet and powerful prayer! Remember the enemies of Jesus cannot make use of prayer, because it must be used in the will and purpose of God. When they lay hold of prayer, however, they are transformed from enemies to friends. Prayer is work! Our battle is to remain strong and not to faint until the answer comes. It is to struggle against the hindrances which would prevent us from continuing in prayer.

We need to be watchful against the temptation to sloth, to feel and suffer with persons or causes that need prayer.

We need to be burden bearers and to be willing for self to be crucified.

In Matthew 9:38 Christ said, 'Pray for the Lord of the harvest to send forth labourers.'

He trained and equipped his disciples for prayer.

In Matthew 18:19 we read, 'If two of you shall agree on earth as touching *anything*, that they shall ask it shall be done for them of my Father which is in heaven.' Again in Matthew 17:20, 'If you have faith like a mustard seed . . . nothing shall be impossible unto you.'

Matthew 21:22 says, 'And all things whatsoever ye ask in prayer believing ye shall receive!' The words 'whatsoever' and 'anything' are all-inclusive. The assurance is that nothing is *impossible*.

We can pray for:

(a) Men 'sent from God' (like John the Baptist) to be in our pulpits instead of sitting idly and accepting whoever comes. There is a danger that some people who go into the ministry should never have gone in. There are those who should be in the ministry but we have not prayed for them to be sent forth. This is the battle. Hell laughs at us. Heaven weeps!

(b) That the 'heathen' be given to us as an inheritance. We should pray that the spirit of prayer will distribute the non-believers in our communities, offices and churches so that as believers we can present them daily and personally to God each day and see them converted.

Ours is to pray that God will send God-fearing young men to our universities to become teachers who will not be neglectful of or harmful to the souls of the children.

Prayer must precede and accompany all work in the Kingdom. Satan wants us not to pray. He allows us to be busy organizing, preaching etc., but without prayer. He knows . . . 'He who plows not in the closet will never reap in the pulpit.'

Jesus is up there but his hand is extended to us so that we on our knees can reach it. His power will flow to us and then to other men. He says, 'Pray without ceasing.' The flesh wars against the Spirit and says: 'I am tired, I am sleepy! I will pray tomorrow.' WE LOSE THE BATTLE!

How then can we develop good habits of consistent prayer life?

Like all other trade, and prayer is the Christian trade – 'practice makes perfect'. We must make specific efforts. However in Zechariah 12:10 God says: 'And I will pour upon the house of David and upon the inhabitants of Jerusalem the spirit of grace and supplication.'

We must keep the spirit of prayer in constant empolyment! He who prays without ceasing is likely to rejoice evermore!

Because the Spirit reveals Jesus to us as the answering Christ, the Holy Spirit is the spirit of prayer. Prayer is a matter of the heart not of the schools, yet the best school in which we learn to pray is PRAYING! Prayer is the best dictionary to define the art and nature of praying. We need to pray more than to be concerned about its definition.

Prayer is the easiest yet hardest of tasks. Prayer is the weakest yet most powerful of activities. It is the most formidable weapon and yet rarely used. We need to practise it and labour and toil at it.

The lazy man *does not*, *will not*, cannot pray, for prayer demands energy.

Paul calls it striving and agony, for Jacob it was wrestling, for the Syrophoenician woman it was a struggle! Sometimes the school of prayer involves trials and suffering. It is then that we learn to be contented to be electric power plants, neither seen or appreciated but carrying a powerful force that brings life and light into lives and homes.

4

God's Power Working in Women

G. MWITI

It has often been said that the hand that rocks the cradle rules the world. It follows that the reverse is also true, that the hand that rocks the cradle wrecks the world.

Which of these will be true for women in Africa as we come towards the close of this century? It is clear that women are co-workers with the Most High, to build with him, or if not, to tear to pieces as instruments in the hands of the lowest – the prince of darkness.

The direction the world takes therefore, the direction that Africa takes – depends on our willingness as women, first to say – 'Yes Lord, I am called to build, to be your co-worker. I will make myself available for you, I will accept your cleansing, so that washed and made holy, your power can flow through me into your world.' There is no short-cut; either I am available or I am not, either I am cleansed or I am not; either I am used of the Lord or of the evil one. Which will it be?

The Bible is full of examples of women who show us clearly that there is no middle course. We have Sarah, the woman of faith, who consented to be God's handmaid, to do the impossible, to break the laws of nature and mother a child at the age of ninety. The Bible says that her secret was to tarry at God's promise until he found her there. She was convinced that he who has promised is able – however long it took, whatever the odds were against her. She tarried at God's promise, and he met her there (Heb. 11:11).

Then, on the other extreme, we have our own mother Eve, the last and the best of God's creation, Eve, blessed with all those wondrous gifts God has given us (Gen. 3). She was not stupid, but a clever woman, who could even talk politics with the Devil. To do what Eve did needed an analytical woman, who was not content to obey blindly. The Devil knew also that we have the gift of curiosity. The fruit indeed looked lovely, and it would make her wise! You see, she even knew that she needed more wisdom! Then, we also have the tongue, God's great gift of conversation that sets us apart from all other creatures And who talks better than the woman?

Then, when we are convinced, how fast we convince others? Many husbands sometimes give way just to save themselves from endless discussions which can even turn into nagging sometimes! So, the Devil knew that he would find Eve with little on her hands, ready to prattle away and ready to quench her curiousity. Man would never have had the patience to argue and talk at such length.

What we are saying here is that the gifts we have are unique and wonderful, yet open to abuse, depending on who becomes Lord and Master of our lives. It is either the creative power of the Creator God in us, or the destructive influence of the evil one. Which will it be for us women of Africa? In which direction shall we direct the affairs of this great continent?

We pray that long-lasting peace shall be the heritage of our children in this Continent, peace flowing from Cape Town to Cairo, from the shores of the Indian Ocean to those of the Pacific. Yet peace is not the result of men's wisdom, it is a gift from God through men and women yielded to the source of all peace. Acts 9:31 – 'Meanwhile, the Church had peace and grew in strength and numbers. The believers *learned to walk in fear* of the Lord and in the comfort of the Holy Spirit.'

What does God see when he looks at Africa today? Does he see a continent after his own heart, a continent that walks in the fear of the Lord? Does he see her as a bride, pure and holy for her bridegroom? In Jeremiah 2, God looked at Israel, the chosen bride of the Lord. He said, 'Israel my beloved, I remember your devotion, the devotion of your youth; your love as a bride, how you followed me in the wilderness in a land not sown.' (v.2).

Israel WAS holy, the first fruits of his harvest.

But now Israel has changed her gods, changed her glory for that which does not profit. She has committed two evils:

– Forsaken me, the fountain of living waters, and
– Built cisterns that cannot hold any water.
THEREFORE
– The showers have been withheld, the spring rain has not come.

What does God see when he looks at us, women of Africa today? Does he see women that are available to be co-workers with God, building with him, right from Jerusalem – our homes, then out to the world at large? God is a God of details, wanting holiness right from my threshhold out to a continental meeting like this one. Has the fear of the Lord, my love for the Lord, my devotion to him – affected my walk with my spouse, my children, my friends, parents, relatives, my employer and colleagues at work? This is because unless I am willing to be a Christian walking in holiness in the details of my life, I cannot be used of the Lord in great things, for 'He who is faithful in very little things will be also be faithful in much . . .' (Luke 16:10).

The Lord tells us today – I have called you to build with me, I have called you to be:-

1. The Light of the World – Matthew 5:14

'Your walk with me will show Africa the way to peace, because peace can be found only in the Prince of Peace.' Lord, is there peace or tumult in my heart today? Still the storm Lord and please, be my peace.

2. The Salt of the Earth – Matthew 5:13

'Your walk with me will preserve the standards of holiness in Africa. Do not imitate anyone else, walk in my love, in my victorious power, for God is able to keep you from falling and to present you holy and blameless in his presence on the final day.' Lord, am I holy? Am I the salt where I live? Do others see the glory of the Lord in me? Break me and build me again Lord, cleanse me and use me.

3. A Spring, A Fountain of Living Waters – John 4:14

'Your walk with me will cause a fountain of living waters to flow in your life for ever. You shall build by causing others to drink of your joy, peace, faithfulness, contentment, holiness. The waters of this world poison and kill, but my stream is the water of life, that strengthens the weak, brings life to the dead and sustains through eternity . . . until I come.' What kind of water do others drink from my life Lord? Is it the water of bitterness, anger and resentment that kills or the water that gives life? If you were to take me home today Lord, what memories of me would others cherish? Cleanse me and use me Lord.

4. You are a Tree Planted by the Riverside – Jeremiah 17:8

'Your walk with me will cause you to be like a tree that is always green even when it passes through the fire, because I am with you always. You and I shall build together, because others will always find fruit in you because your roots will dig deep and draw nourishment from me. You are my hope for Africa, because through you, I will feed many.' Lord, is there fruit on me today? How firmly am I planted in you? Am I only leaves with no fruit? Save me Lord, and bless me with fruit enough to feed others.

5. You are a Rock, a Pillar of Strength – Matthew 16:18

'Because you have chosen to build your life upon me, the Rock of Ages, even you shall be a strong pillar on which others can lean. You will be a predictable woman, a trusted spouse, a trusted friend, a person that others can count upon. Between you and me, broken lives will be put together again as they find their foundation in Jesus Christ.'

Lord, have I been building together with you – in my sharing, prayer life, family life, and professional life, or have I taken pleasure in breaking? Has my family found me available or am I too busy to be a pillar on which others can lean? (My grandmother's hut had a central pillar, supporting the rafters which carried the roof. Through the years, the pillar attained a shiny polished look from the many hands that rubbed on it – some children came crying with muddy hands, looking for comfort from grandma, others enjoyed grandma's boiled beef and afterwards rubbed the fat from their hands on to the pillar, still others with running noses found the pillar a good enough recipient, others with tired feet would lean on the pillar talking to grandma). Such is the pillar you would have me be Lord, ready and available, predictable and supportive and through the ages, I will shine with your glory.

6. You are a Priest – 1 Peter 2:5

'Your walk with me will remind you day by day that you are a holy priesthood, my mediator between others and myself – your family, relatives, church, nation, continent, and indeed the whole world. You, woman of Africa, woman of God – will stand in the gap and intercede for my people. You will intercede for the broken homes of Africa, you will intercede for the orphans left all alone as the cruel hand of civil strife has torn their parents away, you will intercede for the nations torn apart by civil war, you will intercede for those that hunger for food, both physical and spiritual, you will intercede for the leaders of Africa, both in the churches and the Governments represented here today, you will stand in the gap for our youth, swept to and fro by every change of the wind of fashion, for those that are enslaved to immorality and the slowly creeping danger of addictive drugs, you will stand in the gap for the men of Africa, that they shall be men after God's own heart, men that fear and worship me, men that are accountable to me for all they do. Yes, in Jesus' name, you will put to death immorality in my land, you will refuse corruption and bribery, you will build the family unity and pray for any straying husbands and sons to come home.'

Women of Africa, is there anything too hard for our Lord? Indeed no, we shall rise and we shall build together with God. We shall stand in the gap.

7. You are an Ambassador – 2 Corinthians 5:20

'Your walk with me will remind you day by day that you are an ambassador for Christ – God making his appeal through you, beseeching Africa to be reconciled to God.' Am I taking those High Commissioner duties seriously? Have I made it clear what my King wants with men? Is my country, heaven the most important place in my life? If it is, why do I live as if there was another way, except Jesus, to heaven? Why do I worship politics above salvation? Why do I exalt popularity above Christ? Why do I disown my Lord in that executive office? Why do I treat my unsaved friends and relatives as if they are alright without Christ.

Lord, give me a heart that bleeds with you for the sin of your people! Give me a heart that yearns for their salvation! Give me a spirit of urgency in my duties for the Kingdom! Lord, put to death laziness and sloth among the women of Africa, so that we crucify our complacency, our luxuries that would replace Christ, the time-wasting occupations that make us forget your words to be ready at all times, because you are coming soon! Forgive us Lord, women of Africa for those times when we have given our children education, good homes, healthy bodies – and forgotten to give them the most important heritage of all – leading them to a victorious new life in Christ Jesus! Forgive us Lord, women of Africa, when we have fed and clothed the hungry, but not preached the gospel in and out of season. Forgive us for looking after our husbands, meeting their bodily needs day by day, but not praying for them to know you more and serve you. Lord, make me an ambassador for Christ, who is 'not ashamed of the gospel, for it is the power of God for salvation to everyone who believes . . .' (Rom. 1:16).

8. You are a Watchman – Ezekiel 3:17

'Your walk with me will keep you on the alert, to watch over your family, your church, your nation, your continent, indeed, your world as a mother-hen watches over her chicks.' During this conference beloved, we shall discuss issues that affect women in this continent, praying and looking for solutions. We are not taking the job from our men-folk, indeed no! We are complementary parts, to warn them because the Lord, who gives the Spirit of discernment is our God as well.

WHAT WILL OUR TESTIMONY AND OUR MESSAGE BE?

The Lord has taught us that he wants pure vessels, fit for the Master's use as he sets forth to build Africa. He first of all seeks to purify us and then send us out with a complete message to our continent. The Lord reminds us of the following:

1. You shall have NO other gods before me – Exodus 20:3

What is a god? The dictionary defines this as 'someone or something to which excessive attention is paid' – something that competes with God for our attention. What is threatening to displace the worship of the Eternal God in Africa?

God calls us to see the increasing idol-worship in our continent, the rise of the occult and allegiance to gods even of Eastern religions, the worship of materialism, the worship of the power and influence of politics, the increasing self-worship and ego-centricity leading to family break-ups, separation and divorce, even the desire for power and worship of man within the Church of Jesus Christ, often leading to splits and factions in the Church. Put to death idol worship in Africa in the power of the Holy Spirit, then rise and let us build.

2. You shall NOT make for yourself a graven image – Exodus 20:4

The Lord says, 'I am a jealous God, visiting the iniquity of the fathers on the children' to the third and fourth generation. One of my greatest concerns as a Counselling Psychologist is the growing worship of the 'bottle' – alcohol by many of our menfolk. Not that Africa is different from other continents, but men who will not call upon the Lord in the time of stress and consequently change their lifestyle, but who instead seek to drown it all with bottles of alcohol are making this statement to their families – that alcohol is the solution to problems, or that it is in a drinking atmosphere that business contacts are made etc etc.

This distorted sense of manhood is passed on to our sons and daughters, and generations of alcoholics are made. Today, the world over, many women carry the burden of the family because men are away drinking. In other places children are wounded in spirit because of the apathy which results from alcohol. Many deaths on our roads are caused by drunk drivers. Children are abused. You can name other results. It is only the power of the blood of Jesus that can shatter the enslaving power of alcohol, setting the captive free and overcoming the inherited weakness.

3. **Do not take the Name of the Lord in vain . . . Exodus 20:7,**
4. **Remember the sabbath day to keep it holy . . . v. 8,**
5. **Honour your father and mother . . . v. 12,**
6. **You shall not murder . . . v. 13,**
7. **You shall not commit adultery . . . v. 14,**
8. **You shall not steal . . . v. 15,**
9. **You shall not bear false witness against your neighbour . . . v. 16,**
10. **You shall not covet your neighbour's house, ox, wife/husband, or anything that is your neighbour's.**

Africa, what heritage are we passing on to our children? Is it one of holiness and fear and worship of the Lord, or one of emptiness and disregard for our Creator?

God wants to begin right here with us today - to break us, melt us, mould us, fill us and then use us. Am I ready to accept these conditions? Then and then only will God use me to build my home, my church, my nation and my continent. Is this too much for the Lord to ask of us? He can use only cleansed vessels. Have you been there, to the cleansing stream, emptied of self and filled with God? What excuses have you given – 'Lord, you do not know my family. I alone know you. How can I build amidst such opposition?' 'Lord, if you really know the man I married, you will understand that I cannot be a builder. Look how many years I have tried Lord! All in vain. Are you sure you mean me Lord?'

'Then there is my church, so cold and legalistic. I cannot even penetrate it with a prayer, leave aside a testimony. And Lord, myself. I am weak, even in my body Lord, I am also a quiet soft spoken woman. You know I cannot address meetings. All I do is cook for the preachers.' The Lord says – 'I know all that child, but I have called you in righteousness. You are mine. All I need is your willingness to listen to me and to obey me . . ., then leave the rest to me, for I am your inheritance. Sit at my feet and learn of me, for –

I am the Lord.
I have called you in righteousness.
I will also hold your hand and watch over you.
I will appoint you as a covenant to the people.
I will also hold you by the hand and watch over you.
(You and I together will BUILD AFRICA).'

The Lord cautions us that we should never under-estimate our God-given ability to build together with Jesus Christ. Paul writes: 'As God's messenger, I give each of you God's warning: Be honest in your estimate of yourselves, measuring your value by how much faith God has given you' (Rom. 12:3).

It follows then, that my value is directly proportional to my faith. Yielded to God, I can do ALL things through Christ who gives me strength and keeps me humble. And wherever Christ and I shall go, there will be life. For he is the life-giving stream, the river of life, and wherever the river shall flow, there will be life (Ezek. 47:9).

The Lord now, finally calls each one of us to drink once again of this river of life, and Africa will not thirst because you shall take the healing streams wherever we go from here. Have you been there, to the cleansing stream? Have you drunk of the life-giving water? The Lord would have us be washed white, anointed anew and sent back to build with him.

OUR TIME HAS COME, LET US RISE UP AND BUILD!

May our prayer today be:-

Cause me to thirst for Thy River O Lord,
Cause me to thirst for Thy River O Lord,
Cause me to thirst for Thy River O Lord,
Cause me to thirst, cause me to come, cause me to drink.

Cause me to come to Thy River O Lord,
Cause me to come to Thy River O Lord,
Cause me to come to Thy River O Lord,
Cause me to thirst, cause me to come, cause me to drink.

Cause me to drink of Thy River O Lord,
Cause me to drink of Thy River O Lord,
Cause me to drink of Thy River O Lord,
Cause me to thirst, cause me to come, cause me to drink.

Part Two

Our Time Has Come:
Family Issues

5

Paper given at PACWA
– August 9, 1989, Nairobi
Family Life

INGRID TROBISCH

'So do not throw away your confidence; it will be richly rewarded. You need to persevere so that when you have done the will of God, you will receive what he has promised' (Heb. 10:35). This is the word that I would like to give my sisters today when we think of family life.

Thank you for giving me the honour of speaking to this assembly. Even though I am living at present in the United States with my 90-year-old mother and nine brothers and sisters, many of my roots are still in Africa. Eighty years ago my father said 'yes' to the missionary call to come to Africa. In 1919, seventy years ago, he arrived in Nigeria where he served as a pioneer. From there he went to Cameroun and Chad and mapped the regions where there was no gospel witness. Then he was sent to Tanzania, and that is where I was born at Old Moshi on the slopes of Kilimanjaro among the Chagga people. He returned to Tanzania alone during the Second World War and died of malaria in Dar es Salaam in March 1943, leaving my mother a widow with ten children in the United States. She was very brave and said when she heard of his death: 'The future is not dark. God has provided up till now. He will continue to provide.' My mother did not throw away her confidence during those hard years. Before my father returned to Africa in 1942, he was at home for many years because the church had no money to send him back to Africa. When his friend asked him, 'Are you not sorry that you cannot be working on the mission field?' my father replied, 'Don't you see, my family is my mission.' He spent many hours every Sunday teaching us one by one. Twenty years after his death five of his sons and daughters and his widow were serving as missionaries on five different continents.

I remember the day my father explained to me about Mary, the mother of Jesus, and how she became pregnant even though she had never slept with a man. This was a good occasion to explain to me as a young girl the miracle of life. Then he said, 'You are not too young to begin to pray for the young man

41

who will some day be your husband.' I was only nine or ten, but I took his advice very seriously. It was fifteen years later when I met this man, Walter Trobisch, a young pastor in Germany. We were married and served together in French-speaking Cameroun where our five children were born and spent their childhood years. It was during this time that my husband wrote the book, *'I Loved a Girl'*. This little book has been translated into over 70 languages and we have received 15,000 letters from Africans in 40 countries asking for help with their problems about love, sex and marriage. For 25 years my husband and I taught together in Family Life Seminars, wrote books about family life and answered letters from our readers. Then on October 13, 1979, Walter died very suddenly of a heart attack in our little home in the Austrian mountains. We had just returned from a three month missionary trip around the world. And I became a widow, just as my mother had become a widow so many years before. For any of you who have had this experience of losing both a father and a husband, may I give you the word: 'A father to the fatherless, a defender of the widows is God in his holy dwelling' (Ps. 68:18).

WHAT IS THE MESSAGE GOD HAS GIVEN US FOR FAMILY LIFE?

Many of you know it from my husband's book, *'I Married You'*. It is taken from Genesis 2:24: 'For this cause a man shall leave his father and mother, *cleave* to his wife, and the two shall become *one flesh*.'

1. *To leave father and mother means to break with tradition*. It is the same struggle all over the world, not only in Africa. I remember the day before our wedding in Germany, my mother-in-law stood up before our guests and said the following: 'I hereby give the first place in the heart of my son Walter to Ingrid.' I didn't know then what a courageous word she said. I am now a mother-in-law five times over, and each time it is a struggle for me to cut the cord to my son or daugher and give the first place position to their spouse. I call my children-in-law, my children-in-love.

2. *To cleave is another word for love*. It means to be best friends, also to be brother and sister in the Lord at the same time as we are husband and wife. I must never compare my husband's weaknesses with the strengths of another man, especially with the strengths of my father. I remember as a child quarrelling with my brothers and sisters as to which one of us was our father's favourite child. We decided to test my father when he came home from a trip. We all stood in a row and we said to each other: 'When our father gets out of his car, we will see which child he embraces first. That will be his favourite child.' He came home, got out of his car, looked at the row of his children with love in his eyes and said, 'Your mother is first.' When I saw him embracing my mother, I felt safe. I knew it was right that father and mother were closest to each other. Because they were cleaving to each other, all of us children were safe in their marriage tent. Parent-effectiveness depends upon partner-effectiveness. As one father wrote in a poem:

'Thank you Lord, for children brought to life because we loved. Lord of life, keep us loving, so that they may grow up whole in love's overflow' (Joseph Bayley, *Psalms of Life*).

3. *Becoming One Flesh*. Sex is a wonderful gift of God. A book entitled *Christian, Celebrate Your Sexuality* was recently published. The Bible begins with the body, creation, and it ends with the body, resurrection. We should not be ashamed to call those organs by name which God was not ashamed to create.

Children come out of the one-flesh union. I believe that there is no greater moment in the life of a married couple than when they can lovingly and knowingly call into being a new life. In order to do this we need to be able to recognize in our cycle, those days when we are fertile and the days when we are infertile.

At our Family Life Seminars we always taught our couples this little song to the tune of Brother John (Frere Jacques):

Watch your cycle, Watch your cycle.
Write it down, Write it down.
Menses, early dry days,
Fertile time, late dry days.

WHAT IS FAMILY LIFE EDUCATION?

Family life education means first of all: helping men and women understand each other physically, emotionally and spiritually.

Secondly: giving help to parents who want to raise their children wisely and prepare them for a healthy adulthood.

Thirdly: making a change in our society through healthily contagious family (and single) living.

For us women it means that we are the 'keepers of the springs', the educators of our children. Who else will teach them *absolute chastity before marriage* and *absolute fidelity in marriage*?

We need to teach our young people that nobility is the ability to say 'No' and that 'two warm bodies do not heal a lonely heart.' As my friend and co-worker, Grace Kimathi of Kenya says: 'Marriage does not bring fulfillment to unfulfilled people.' Our goal is to 'release couple power' and that means a whole woman plus a whole man and together they will be a great source of power. One plus zero does not equal two.

We will hear an exhaustive paper on AIDS. I would just like to comment that AIDS is leading us into a conservative society. In the United States, our society is not prepared for the epidemic of broken women caused by abortion. Please sisters, don't let it happen in Africa, that a mother's womb becomes her baby's tomb.

May I say a word about single women. At the close of one of our Family Life Seminars where both married and single people attended, our Ethiopian co-worker said: 'We are all married to Christ. There is only the difference between the one-person couples and the two-person couples.' My son Daniel, a Christian psychologist says, 'There is only one thing harder than living alone and that is to live with another person.' 'Only the one who has learned to live successfully alone is able to make a success of marriage.' Derek Prince in his book, *God is a Matchmaker* writes: 'Celibacy is like damming a river. If the river of sex is dammed, a corresponding greater volume of spiritual, intellectual and emotional energy may be released to other forms of expression – such as intercession, scholarship, artistic creativity, or service to the poor. Surrender of the sex drive breaks its tyranny and power . . . People who do the greatest work in the world are strongly-sexed people who subordinate sex to the ends for which they live . . . Remember the strongly-sexed can strongly serve.'

To solve a problem, you don't keep bailing water out of the boat. You repair the hole. The parents are the first and foremost family life educators and their role begins long before the birth of a child. A wise man said that if you want to bring up a child in the right way, you must begin 25 years before the child is born. Is a child thought of principally as an inheritor, one to carry on the family name and tradition? Or is he thought of as a very real person to be loved and trained to grow up as a healthy individual to make a worthy contribution to both family and country?

The time of pregnancy is all-important. The attitude of the mother towards her unborn child is already absorbed by that child and can later affect the child's personality and self-esteem. The chief of the Chagga tribe, where I was born on the slopes of Kilimanjaro, has put it correctly when he tells his men: 'Take good care of the pregnant woman. She is the most important person in our tribe.' She is carrying the future in her womb. A positive attitude towards childbirth can be our greatest help against abortion.

The moment of birth should be the hour of the woman's greatest dignity, when she is a co-worker with the Creator in bringing new life into the world. At no time is the support of her husband more necessary. (I do not think that Joseph left Mary alone in the hour of birth when our Saviour was born.) At the moment of birth, the young couple becomes a family. In the hour after birth, the child is bonded to his mother and should be also to his father. My oldest son wrote to me recently after his wife had given birth to their first child: 'Betty had a long and hard labor. It took the same amount of energy for her to bring forth our child as it would to climb one of the highest mountains in Austria. Never has my respect been so great for a person as it was for my wife at the hour of birth. The experience of holding little Michael Walter and giving him his first bath was indescribable. We are bonded for life.'

Newborn babies need three things: food, warmth and security. They receive all three at their mother's breast and the mother is laying a foundation for that mutual confidence and companionship from which all that is best in human nature develops. Every woman needs a 'Doula' which means 'someone who mothers the mother'. Every caregiver needs care herself. If a mother is allowed to develop a strong relationship to her small child, many problems of educating and raising that child later on will be eliminated. Solnit has said, 'All the experts in the world concerned with infants and their parents cannot make up for one good parent.'

The father is the first man that the daughter knows. Her relationship to him and the way he acts as a father will determine to a great extent her attitude towards men later in her life. Also her relationship to her heavenly Father will often depend upon her relationship to her earthly father. It is important that we as parents be role models for our children. The father is the role model for his son. The daughter needs a mother with whom she can identify. Sex education begins at the age of two months, when the baby is already able to absorb the atmosphere existing between his parents. A wise psychologist gives this advice to fathers: 'If you want to love your child, then love the child's mother.' And I would like to say to all mothers, 'If you want to love your child, love your child's father.'

It is the father who provides the direction, who takes hold of the hand of his young child and introduces him to the outside world. He also establishes the limits. A child must learn that, if he oversteps these boundaries, he has to accept the consequences, and this includes fair punishment. It is the mother who furnishes warmth and light for the small child.

The school years are the time to integrate the family cultures of both sides. The child's sense of identity and self-esteem are strongly formed through this information.

During the adolescent years the parents may teach their children that it is possible to live a fulfilled life in spite of many unfulfilled desires. An African chief once told his son, 'Only a baby wants what he wants when he wants it. A real man can wait.' All young people, in order to become mature adults, go through three stages in their love relationships: the **auto-erotical** stage, when they are in love with themselves and project this love image to their partners; the **homo-erotical** stage, when they can have deep boy-boy friendships and girl-girl friendships without any genital sexual expression; and the **hetero-erotical** stage, which is the mature love relationship between a man and a woman. It is important to help adolescents understand their own development and to show them the goal of marriage with a mature partner. A German author has said: 'He who wants to be happy should not get married, only the one who wants to make his partner happy. He who wants to be understood should not get married, only the one who is ready to understand his partner.'

Here are some suggestions which my late husband wrote many years ago as arguments in talking to young people about the folly of pre-marital sexual relations. Walter wrote:

1. One cannot try marriage by having sex. It is like trying death by sleeping very hard or trying out a parachute from a third-storey window.

2. To learn by doing means not the satisfaction of a desire, but the mastering of it.

3. A boy becomes effeminate by giving in to every desire, but masculine by resisting. A good girl want a man who respects her and is ready to wait for marriage.

4. A boy will never get sick because of abstention, but he can easily do damage to himself physically and psychologically by indulging in premarital relations.

5. There is a truth in the theory of 'learning by doing' but only with one's own wife. 'To enrich oneself too quickly will often impoverish' is an African proverb.

6. If a boy is afraid of mockery and insult, he should think of Jesus, who has been mocked and insulted for him. Christ is the only one who can make him a man.

7. By having premarital relations he does irreparable damage to himself and to the girl. A Swiss theologian has said: 'The girl receives an indelible imprint from the first man to whom she gives herself. She will not be able to detach her thoughts from him, even if she hates him when she later marries the one she loves.' and 'Sexual adventures before marriage can awaken in the

young man a polygamous instinct, a taste for change, which will endanger his future marriage in advance.' Benjamin Franklin has said: 'Marriage without love leads to love without marriage.'

We need a new theology of marriage which points out that children are not the only purpose of marriage, but that the fellowship between husband and wife is a fulfillment in itself. Instead of basing our argument on the commandment, 'You shall not commit adultery,' we should rather base it on two others. The first is, 'You should not steal.' As long as a girl does not belong to any man she belongs to God or as one African student has said: 'On the marrige day the man receives his wife from God's hand as Adam received Eve in the garden where they lived alone. In knowing your wife before marriage you are like a child stealing from its father.'

The other relevant commandment is: 'You shall love your neighbour as yourself.' Since both the girl and the boy are hurt by premarital intercourse, this commandment is transgressed. But this again shows that all our teaching about marriage in Africa depends upon a new interpretation of Christian love.

After a new seminar in Europe a young Frenchman said to Walter: 'Am I not right, the whole subject of marriage is for you an excuse to evangelize?' His answer: 'For me marriage is the best landing strip of the gospel in our times.'

6

Divorce

FEMI NJIE

INTRODUCTION

Divorce is an issue about which for a long time many have been silent but which is gradually destroying the very fabric of many societies. Even the Christian church has to some extent wrongly remained silent. Today, the church has to grapple with this issue as on one hand many divorced persons become converted and join the church and on the other there are believers who have sought and are seeking divorce.

It is important that this issue is examined critically under God so that with a balanced biblical approach we can find lasting solutions to the problem.

Before we can talk about divorce it is important that we look first very briefly at marriage. Today there are so many different types and forms of marriage that it would be best to go back to the beginning and find out what the author of marriage intended it to be. It must be remembered that marriage was not man-ordained. It was God who first designed marriage as a fundamental element of all human society. God's will for marriage is found in the pages of the Bible – a man shall leave his mother and father and cleave to his wife. Secondly, marriage is a foundational institution. Society itself depends on marriage. Thirdly, marriage is not primarily for procreation. The propagation of the human race is a sub-purpose of marriage. Marriage is something more than mating.

The major reason for marriage was to solve the problem of loneliness. Marriage was established because Adam was alone and that was not good. Companionship, therefore, is the essence of marriage. On the other hand it must be noted that there are some to whom God has given the gift of living single for a purpose.

Divorce cannot be fully understood unless companionship in marriage is fully understood. In biblical days the Engagement was an important event. Even though the couple did not come together they were regarded as man and wife and there was no room for illicit sexual relations. The penalty was death by stoning or a letter of divorce. It is worth noting that a marriage which did not begin with a sexual union (Matt. 1:25) was going to be ended by divorce.

Marriage, therefore is a covenant of companionship. It is a formal arrangement between two persons to become companions for life. The marriage union by covenant solves the problem of loneliness not merely by filling a gap but by overfilling it. The marriage union is the closest, most intimate of all human relationships. God's revealed goal for a husband and wife is to become one in all areas of their relationship – intellectually, emotionally and physically – the covenant of companionship.

The Companionship aspect must be stressed. Marriage is not only a building block of society and the church but occupies a key place in human life. Difficulties arise when a man or a woman puts activities, things, achievements, business or other persons in the place that God has accorded his or her spouse or family. In our modern society, a man or a woman may become so concerned about his/her work or qualification that he or she becomes separated from his/her spouse for a very long period. This is a sure breeding ground for the evil one. In another situation a man may allow his mother to rule his home. Imagine the kind of tension that will be stirred up in that home. The man has forgotten the cleaving aspect of marriage which will result in perfect companionship. Divorce will be a foreign element in a marriage where true and perfect companionship exists. Divorce is always the result of sin. Under God the husband and wife must put each other first. A marriage lacking companionship is heading towards the misery of divorce. All that destroys companionship must be avoided.

WHAT IS DIVORCE?

According to Jary Adams in his book *Marriage, Divorce and Remarriage in the Bible*, divorce can be defined as the repudiation and breaking of that covenant in which both parties vowed to provide companionship in all its ramifications for one another.

The word divorce means 'cut off' (Deut. 24:1–4; Isa. 50:1; Jer. 3:8) or 'put away'. In the New Testament the word means to loose form, put away, send, release or dismiss and to separate. The modern view of separation (without reconciliation or divorce) falls short of biblical teaching.

DIVORCE IN THE BIBLE

Contrary to some opinions the concept of divorce is biblical. The Bible recognizes and regulates divorce. The believer must therefore understand it and teach what God says in his Word. The origin of divorce is, however, unknown. Unlike marriage divorce was never instituted by God but by human beings. There is nothing to show in the Scriptures that divorce was instituted by God. Jesus emphasizes in Matthew 19:8 – from the beginning it was not so. The practice was allowed by Moses because of the hardness of people's hearts.

The Bible is not silent on the subject of divorce nor does it always condemn it. God says in Malachi 2:16 that he hates divorce. In Jeremiah 3:8 God however says that because of Israel's backsliding and adultery he had given her a bill of divorce. God hates divorce but more so what causes every divorce. Even the results that often affect children and injured parties of a divorce will not stop him from willing divorce (Ezr. 10). God hates divorce on ground which he has not sanctioned.

A balanced biblical attitude towards divorce is important – hating all the things that God hates while recognizing that in this sinful world divorce is possible. There are, however, many wrong attitudes in some conservative churches. From the way divorcees are treated one would think that they have committed the unpardonable sin. *It must be made clear, however that those who obtained divorce wrongfully must not be excused for what they have done.* Those who divorce on unbiblical grounds are committing sin against a holy God.

THE PROCESS OF DIVORCE

In biblical terms, how did divorce take place? There is more detail in this area than even engagement or wedding ceremonies.

Deuteronomy 24:1–4 outlines the three-step procedure:

1. There was a Bill of Divorce which protected the one who received it from false accusations as it clearly set forth her status as unmarried.
2. The Bill must be served – the one divorcing personally puts the bill into the hand of the one who is being divorced.
3. The person divorced must be sent from the home.

Points Noted from the Bill

1. Formal public documents signed by witness stood as a legal record.
2. The bill effected a permanent separation, thus relieving the parties from the covenant of companionship, expressly giving the divorcee the right to remarry.

It must be reiterated that God hates divorce. He did not institute it. He only recognizes it and regulates it under biblically prescribed circumstances.

BELIEVERS AND DIVORCE

In general, the Christian's position is that divorce is never desirable. Reconciliation is always possible for believers. Even the passage in Deuteronomy meant that people had to think twice before divorce – a man who had divorced his wife could never have had her back again once she had married someone else.

The New Testament forbids divorce among believers except on two grounds. Jesus himself acknowledged one ground of divorce among believers and this is fornication or sexual sin. Jesus clearly stated that adultery is committed by remarriage unless the first wife was put away for fornication (Matt. 19:9). Some think that fornication here refers to the engagement period and for others fornication is being used interchangeably with adultery. Scripture writers used the word fornication to describe sexual sin in general. It refers to incest (1 Cor. 5:1); homosexuality (Jude 7) and even adultery (Jer. 3:1, 2, 6, 8). Adultery is more than sexual sin. The marriage covenant is always in view. Committing adultery by fornication simply means that by engaging in sexual sin a woman violated her covenant commitment to her husband. Jesus' permission to divorce a spouse is based on the violating act, not on its effect. Even though divorce is permitted, it may not be required as the husband or wife may forgive the sinning partner. Divorce of a believing spouse must be restricted to those who refuse to repent of their sin and decide to persist in sin.

Paul further emphasizes Jesus' point about divorce in his letter to the Corinthians (1 Cor. 7:10–11) by stating that neither a Christian man nor a woman should divorce each other. He commands the wife not to separate from her husband. This separation is actually divorce because he goes on to say that if she does separate she should remain unmarried so that there can be some reconcilatiation.

Paul also brings out a second ground for divorce. (1 Cor. 7:12–16). In this case an unbelieving spouse seeks to be divorced from a believing spouse. The believer can do everything possible to make the marriage work. In the process, the unbelieving spouse may become converted. If the unbelieving spouse does not agree and he wants to get out of the marriage, divorce is an acceptable alternative. The believing spouse is not bound as long as he or she did not provoke the unbelieving spouse. In the case of a believer married to an unbeliever there cannot be the same insistence on reconciliation as both of them do not have the same resources – God's Word and his Holy Spirit. This is one instance in which divorce is required. In this case the believer is not bound but become freed. The main reason behind this decision is so that peace can prevail.

DIVORCE IN CONTEMPORARY TIMES

In the world today, the divorce rate is getting higher and higher everyday. One would have thought that with higher education, the divorce rate would get lower and lower but the opposite is true. Many marriages are short lived – couples get divorced for unbiblical reasons such as incompatibility, cruelty, in-law interference and so on. This state of affairs is found even among believers which is very sad. The number of broken homes turning out maladjusted children is soaring daily. Moral standards have dropped so badly that in many cases the stigma of divorce no longer exists. Many enter marriage with the thought that if it does not work out, divorce will be an easy way out. Is there no hope? With the rise of Islam and its polygamous tendency, divorce is commonplace. Divorce, it must be remembered, was never an option when God instituted marriage. All divorces stem from sin. If this is the case there is hope!

OUR RESPONSE

What then is our response as evangelical Christian women? Now is the time to get involved. Let us get informed about divorces – causes of, effects of and remedies for (a closer examination will be given to these areas in group discussions). Let us be involved in nipping this bad situation in the bud by being examples ourselves in our marriages. (Remember that marriage is a covenant of companionship). We can also be used of God to organize Prayer and Bible study groups for women setting up marriage counselling centres, reaching out to unbelieving women, and young girls and even divorcees. Many divorces stem from ignorance and the making of choices not ordained by God. A careful study of God's Word, his will for marriage and a complete surrender to God and his will appears to be the solution to this very biting issue. Wrong attitudes towards divorcees should be altered as we willingly examine each situation in the light of God's Word and counsel with them.

Evangelical women of Africa, our time has come to work with God in restoring every nation to his ideal for marriage and family life. May God grant that we shall not be found wanting!

7

In-laws and the Extended Family

FLORENCE ZIUMBE

Marriage can be the most happy or unhappy experience in all life. God's plan for a home life is that it be different from the turmoil that is experienced in the world. He wants the home to be a haven of love, where the husband, wife and children live with a sense of security and a feeling of acceptance. With all the turmoil and violence outside the home, everyone needs a place in life where he is surrounded by peace and love. God ordained the home to be that place of emotional security.

Everyone who marries wants that type of home but a happy home does not just happen.

For the newly weds, there are many areas requiring adjustment in their lives, and one such area is their relationship with their inlaws and their extended family. For us blacks in particular, largely because of historical and cultural factors, the inlaw problem has caused unhappiness and in many cases, the downfall of marriages. It is an area which requires a great deal of care in tackling, and perhaps even requires thorough preparation before marriage. I say this because many of us are deceived into a false sense of security by the initial reception we receive from inlaws before settling down into our marriages.

Your relationship with your partner's family is important. As a Christian, you especially have a responsibility to maintain a healthy relationship with members of your partner's family as a testimony of the power of Christ in daily life.

LIVE SEPARATELY

Occasionally a partner's parents will be so ideal that you never have problems with them, but, frankly, that is an exception rather than the rule. Most parents find it difficult to cut all apron strings after their children marry. It is therefore absolutely necessary after marriage that a couple live separately from their parents.

This is of the utmost importance. The Bible confirms this by stating that for

52

this cause shall a man leave his father and mother and shall cleave to his wife (Matt. 19:5). There has to be a leaving. This, if anything, makes it easier for the parents to accept the fact of their children being adults and starting a family of their own where they can make independent and competent decisions on matters affecting their own lives. If the couple remains in the same home with the parents, who have cared for a partner for over twenty or thirty years in some cases, it is difficult for the parents to relinquish the interest and control which has existed over these years. Further, it would be expecting too much to hope to make your own independent decisions about a home which does not belong to you. You cannot really blame parents who insist on certain rules being maintained in their own home.

It happens, invariably, that in-laws or relatives come to live with a couple in their own home because of health, age or other reasons. When this happens, which is often, the parents should not expect to resume parental control, but should take a submerged role.

I cannot give a better example than that set in the Bible where a young woman, Ruth left her family, her homeland, her religious beliefs to devote herself to her mother-in-law Naomi.

Naomi earned the loyalty and love of Ruth. If you look closely you will see that Naomi achieved this by submerging her personal interests in deference to Ruth. She ordered her life in a pattern which helped the younger generation. Likewise, when the parents of a partner live with you, although members of the family, they remain as your guests, ready to follow and accept the rules of that home and not to superimpose themselves on that family.

I know of many homes which are under great strain because there are too many relatives on extended visits. The most unfortunate aspect of this is that you cannot enquire how long they will be staying, nor are you warned of their extended visit. Added to this, the economics of our present society do not allow us to depart from our budgets substantially. Such concerns though, cannot be shared with your visitors. A climate is created where the couple can become prisoners in their own home as they are not left alone nor get time to concentrate on their own plans or their own family. There is also a crisis of expectations on the parents' part. They feel jealous that their child has been taken away by the marriage. Some expect certain behaviour from the bride and a failure to conform to this may result in gossip and the resultant breakdown in communications.

This always has the most unfortunate results. In this type of situation it is important for the husband to assume a meaningful role of leader in the home – if it is the family of the wife interfering, she must do the telling. Great tact is required to convey the family's reservations without affecting delicate relationships.

If the husband does not take the lead, you become insecure leading to accusations that the husband is preferring his relatives to you. I would suggest the following:-

1. Not many are lucky to have husbands who will be quick to restore the status quo. You should be patient with your husband and you should take care not to speak negatively of your inlaws to your partner. There is a vast difference between an open discussion of existing problems with your husband and negative commenting.

2. You should not be too quick to judge. You may in fact be part of the problem in the puzzle. Remember that it has taken your husband many years to establish his relationship and bonding with his parents and relatives. This is why fighting your husband's relatives without his support is invariably, if not always, fighting a losing battle. The same applies to your husband. We need to accept that on marriage, there is still a lot we need to learn of our partner. It is really the beginning of a long road of education about your partner. It is therefore very unwise on our part to start having differences with inlaws before our husbands know us sufficiently to be able to defend and support us.

   Your husband can best defend you when you knows you well. If he knows you are kind and generous, he can defend against an accusation that you were mean and left them to starve! He can give you his support only when he trusts you and knows that you mean well. Remember without his support, your cause is lost.

3. We must be tolerant and patient. (I can do all things through Christ who strengthens me (Phil. 4:13)) You should be respectful towards both your inlaws. It is most natural for parents to offer advice based on their 20 or more years of experience and sometimes we rebel at this even to the point of rejecting good advice because it comes from one of the parents. On many occasions suggestions are made with good intentions. You can afford to be considerate to your partner's parents. After all, they spent many years and thousands of dollars preparing him for you! The least we can do is to treat them with dignity and respect.

4. Please appreciate that most inlaws' attitudes originate from our culture. Most of our mothers were brought up to believe that daughters in-law should live with them or perform certain duties for them. My mother has repeatedly told me that daughters in-law are there to be looked at and not to be heard. We all know that what you have been brought up to believe in is not very easy to depart from. We must therefore be patient with them because the attitudes are not so much of their own making but to a great extent dictated by the society of the day.

   You will be amazed to find that out of the thousands of us who are here today, many of us will not escape from these ancient beliefs.

5. Tension is normal in any home and to any relationship. It happens between husband/wife, father/son, mother/son, brother/brother, sister/sister. It is therefore not unusual to have differences with your inlaws. It is normal to every relationship. If both parties adopt this attitude to their differences, making up should also happen in the normal course of things and it should not call for walkouts or the vows 'not to step into his/her home ever'. As a Christian you should have a better attitude, being able to apologize first. You can only benefit from such an attitude.

FINANCES AND THE EXTENDED FAMILY

We have a scriptural mandate to provide for those of our own household. Both the Old and New Testament teach that parents are to be loved, supported and cared for. (Exodus 20:12; Leviticus 20:9; James 2:14–20; 1 Timothy 5:8).

Please note that this scriptural injunction applies to both 'spouses' ' families.

We are fortunate that in our upbringing, our culture has been our greatest teacher in the lesson of giving. Africans love giving to their relatives. It's in their nature. The difficulty in marriage is a tendency to favour one family over the other. This always brings tension.

I do not believe that the giving should be completely determined by need – both families must be given, with the amount depending on the need of each family, and, of course, on the couples' resources. However, a total denial to a partner's family because there is no need is likely to result in some tension between the partners.

CONTRIBUTION BY EXTENDED FAMILY

I cannot find a better example of meaningful contribution than that set by our forefathers. All relatives were welcome to the family home because the greater the numbers the greater the contribution in the fields. Each person had something to contribute, be it in the fields, herding cattle, cooking food or fetching firewood. For some reason the extended family today reverses the position and looks to one person as the sole breadwinner, and worker in the family.

Some relatives will expect a working wife to return home and take up cooking duties because it is part of her duties culturally. This is unfortunate. Each person must contribute, in the garden, in the home, and of course, where they are employed, in money. Again, any talking should be done by the offspring who knows the relative better.

Finally, difficulties in family relationships should be talked over openly and lovingly. In cases where a couple cannot compromise their position with dissatisfied relatives, the issues have to be committed to the Lord in prayer, as with all matters in Christian living. Loving people will probably help to restore peace in due time. Bridges can be built over most troubled waters where Christ is the motivator.

8

Polygamy

ESME CHOMBO

WHAT IS MARRIAGE?

In order to understand polygamy fully with all its ills, one needs to have a fairly reasonable knowledge of what marriage is. It is for this reason that I first give a brief definition of marriage.

In simple legal terms, marriage is a mutual agreement between two people of the opposite sex to enter into a union (or a contract). Under the English law (which most commonwealth countries have adopted) in order to contract a valid marriage, it must be shown that either spouse is either single, legally divorced or widowed. It is therefore a union of two people to the exclusion of all others.

Under almost all customary law however, marriage takes on a different complexion altogether – it is an agreement to enter into marriage between a man and one or more women.

Rev. John Stott in his exposition to the All Souls Church in England, preached in 1966 gave four characteristics of a marriage when he spoke on 'The Biblical Doctrine of Marriage'. He stated that marriage is an exclusive union between a man and a woman which has no room for polygamy or promiscuity and it excludes all others.

According to God's divine plan the marriage pact joins one man to one woman; which pact is symbolized by the single rib that was removed from Adam's side with which God formed woman. The Bible makes it very clear that it is God's will that one man should be joined to one woman only (Gen. 2:24; 1 Tim. 3:2).

Apart from what customary law offers us, it can be said that marriage is a permanent and unique covenant that two people of the opposite sex enter into to the exclusion of all others. It is a fellowship of the two people that cannot be attained by any other partnership, that is, not man and man, or man and beast, or woman and woman.

In God's divine plan 'the fitting partner/helper' that he made for man was of such a nature that she would be one with the man and this is what gives marriage its permanent characteristic – for what had become one could not be separated.

The Bible compares the marriage union to that between God and the children of Israel (in the past) and in the future to Christ and the Church. Those who have accepted Christ as Lord and Saviour are regarded as the bride whilst Christ is the bridegroom.

POLYGAMY

Polygamy is a legal, social and psychological evil that women of today need to address their minds to closely and critically. Polygamy has thrived in our society because of various reasons – greed, the permissiveness of our customary law, selfishness, exploitation of the women folk with the consent of the women themselves, marriage at any cost for example, marriage regarded as a form of security e.g. financial – a name for oneself, protection etc.

Only the English law (or adopted English law) has made great strides to address itself to the issue of polygamy by prescribing what can and cannot constitute marriage, that is, the status of the spouse – it stresses singlehood. But polygamy is a social and psychological problem for the following reasons:

(a) It denies/rejects the divine plan of God and it is the same as idolatry or adultery.
(b) It creates unhealthy competition between the wives as they strive for the place of eminence in the man's life.
(c) It destroys the character of a person. We see this in the story of Rachel and Leah. Rachel who was once the beautiful girl who stole Jacob's heart at the well was turned into a monster always out to grasp the man and prevent him from going over to Leah. It creates a lack of trust in the other woman and the husband himself.
(d) It brings bitterness against the other wife/wives and creates a lack of self confidence in oneself. For example, Leah never gained confidence in herself as a person as she knew that her husband openly loved Rachel and so she gave herself to Jacob as an instrument of child bearing with the hope of winning his confidence, but to no avail. It is clear she rated herself as a second class person.
(e) It creates tension in the home between husband and wives, wife and wife, and the children of one woman with those of another, and even one wife and the children of another wife. She regards them as usurpers of her rights and those of her children. As a result, it blinds them to all the beauty of marriage as intended by God. The marriage union is filled with fear, mistrust, jealous and lack of unity and no longer reflects the peace, love and unity of God above. This causes the members to be insensitive to each other's needs and unresponsive to God's Word.
(f) It infringes on one's privacy and can destroy the sexual relationship of a man and his wife. Every time the man sleeps with one woman the woman can fantasize about all sorts of things that happen when the same man and the other wife/wives have sex – thus inhibitions can start building up that will prevent the two from having a fulfilling sexual relationship. For it was meant by God that man and woman, as husband and wife should meet

each other's sexual needs and have a fulfilling sexual life. Sex is clean and God created it for a purpose.

There is need therefore that our societies be made aware of the fact that polygamy is sin and God abhors it and will punish all those who indulge in the same. People must be shown the original and pure purpose of marriage. Men and women of our society need to be biblically instructed about the need to follow God's precepts at any cost despite what custom dictates. The polygamist must however be brought to Christ Jesus who alone can resolve this issue. They must not feel rejected but they need to be made aware of the teaching of the Word of God.

Part Three

Our Time Has Come:
Social Issues

9

Social Injustice

MARY DIJA OGEBE

COMPARE

'Women constitute *half* the world's population, perform nearly *two-thirds* of its work hours, receive *one-tenth* of the world's income and own less than *one-hundredth* of the world's property.'

UNITED NATIONS REPORT 1980

'A woman who fears (honours) the Lord, she shall be praised. Give her the product (fruit, reward) of her hands and let her works praise her in the gate (of her city, town, country).'

PROVERBS 31:30–31

INTRODUCTION

By the term 'social injustice' we are referring to unfair or heavily biased treatment meted out to an individual or a specific group of people by the society in which they live. In this context we shall consider the African woman. The society is the African setting in which they have been born. We are here representing various cultures in Africa, from the East, the West, the South and the North. There are many things common in all Africa such as tribal groupings, lack of technology, subsistence farming, polygamy and spiritism. Discrimination against women is found world-wide and has led to the formation of the Women's Liberation Movement. In the Third World the suffering is so great that no movement can solve it – only the liberty that is found in trusting and serving Jesus. We shall examine the contrasts later.

Let us examine some examples from the *SECULAR* set-up which may be allowed, tolerated or even encouraged by some church leaders.

1. Patrilineal Society

Most tribes in Africa practise patrilineage, ie. children belong to the man and inherit the father's property. Thus giving birth to a boy is preferable to bearing daughters. The birth of too many girls is blamed on the mother and often results in polygamy.

2. Labour Force

Because we lack technology, human resources are very much valued by the African man. The wife is seen as property. She is expected to work hard and to produce other forms of labour through bearing children. She is equivalent to a field! She is hardly worth more than that. She is useful if much is reaped from her so there are special celebrations at the birth of her 10th child. She is quietly and easily discarded if she is not productive. Again the more sons she bears, the more valuable she is as if she had any power to determine any of these. Medically we know better. Women are medically neutral while the man's sperm determines the sex of the baby right from the day of fertilization, ie. before full conception (implantation of the fertilized ovum).

In actual manual work the number of women bears no relationship to what they get out of the harvest. In fact, they expect no pay and have no opportunity to express their feelings. Instead the African woman is denied many basic rights. Oh, how I praise the Lord for Christianity!

3. Denial of Rights

The woman is denied the right to express her feelings, her feeling of hurt. Her opinion is not sought and if she dares to give it it is hardly ever considered. A courageous, outspoken woman has expressed her hurt feelings and the result has been discipline (she has been fined, disowned, insulted). In our modern days women are still being denied

    education
    leadership positions
    rights of inheritance
    opportunities to develop expertise
    chance to distinguish themselves.

Women are regarded as having less status than children, hence the beating and various abuses.

Marriage

This is determined for the woman so that she has no choice in any of the following–

    a) the timing
    b) her partner
    c) the termination
    d) the type (monogamous or polygamous)

Some marriages are such that the woman seems to have been outrightly sold to her husband who may be the age of her grandparents. As a result she is sexually starved. Unfaithfulness can earn the woman severe penalties but never the man. In fact, he is congratulated and praised for extramarital affairs!

5. Employment

Not only is there discrimination in job placements but to get to a top management position women have to work twice or even three times as hard as men. The same is required to retain the post.

The pay may be the same for men and women now but allowances are either denied or given only grudgingly to women. This is based on the erroneous belief that a woman puts in less effort than a man (office work is equated with farm work) and because a woman is often away from work because of pregnancy or her children's ill health. My question always is, 'Whose baby is it? Whose name will it bear – a man's family name or the woman's own? Why should the woman go on maternity leave on half-pay? Is the child to be born not a contribution to the whole society?' (This is without prejudice to family planning and population control. As a child of God and despite my faith I do not believe that contraception is against the will of God. I will preach it any day the Lord grants me the opportunity.)

6. Litigation

Maybe in this field women receive the least and worse attention. My husband and I have agonized when we cannot take in a battered woman with badly neglected children for fear of a worse response from the husband and law enforcement agents. In Africa social welfare is not as effective as the extended family system in settling marital problems so where the man fails to listen to the elders or if the latter team up with him against the wife, the police and the courts (native/area, magistrate and high courts are her last resort). Here the majority of the officers are men and will invariably side with the husband. (Oh, Lord I know you are aware and you are recording everything in your Book of Life. Be merciful to all of us since your mercies endure for ever.)

These are some of the highlights of the injustices experienced in the secular society. What of the *CHURCH* set-up? Are Christian freed from the problems of this kind of prejudice? I wish I could give an emphatic 'Yes' but I cannot. Nevertheless the gospel has delivered us from

a) the stigma of being a woman and therefore *less* than a man,
b) polygamy,
c) being only a piece of property,
d) lack of inheritance etc.

Despite this, in the evangelical set-up, women still receive minimal injustice in the following areas:

1. The Silent Majority

Almost all congregations consist of more women than men but they are silenced. (Boards of elders and executive committees consist of men only.)

2. Spiritual Talents Suppressed

Women are not allowed to develop their spiritual gifts in certain fields which are regarded as purely masculine.

3. Menial Jobs

However, menial jobs like sweeping the church hall or other cleaning are readily passed down to the women. Praise God that we do these jobs unto the Lord and not unto men.

What should the Christian response be to both secular and church-based social injustices? Should they be fought or tolerated? Is there any place for 'Woman's Lib' in the life of the African Christian woman? If she fights will she succeed and if so, how soon? Christ's victory is ours and it will lead to social justice. Christ has conquered Satan and all his repressive plans for society.

Jesus has spoken comforting words to and about women. He said to the woman arrested by the Jewish leaders: 'Neither do I condemn you; go your way. From now on, sin no more' (Jn. 8:11).

God speaks about marriage through the apostle Paul. 'For this cause a man shall leave his father and his mother and shall cleave to his wife, and the two shall become one flesh. Consequently they are no longer two but one flesh. What therefore God has joined, let no man separate.'

Jesus responded to all who came to him. He commended the woman with the alabaster box of ointment. He praised the faith of the woman who touched the hem of his garment as he praised the faith of the Roman centurion. He spoke to the woman of Samaria. I have no doubt but that he commends every African woman who humbly turns to him for help.

From other scriptures we learn the value God places on women. Proverbs 31:30–31 says that the woman who fears God is to be praised and given the reward she has earned.

The apostle Peter tells his readers to honour women because they are the weaker sex (1 Pet. 3:7).

In Romans 8:17 we are called children of God and joint-heirs with Christ. Paul does not say, 'with the exception of women and girls'.

Romans 8:26–27 tells us that the Holy Spirit intercedes for the saints (a word in scripture that embraces both men and women).

We can compare this with the African Masquerade Festival which is for men only.

Women must not eat (only taste).
Women must run and hide or be thoroughly flogged by the 'spirit'.
Women are deprived of the comfort of extra meat but must do all the work.
Left-overs can be discarded or given to the boys but not to women.

But according to 2 Corinthians 10:4 our warfare is not against flesh and blood so we cannot use carnal methods. Therefore joining Women's Lib is out of the question. Even if the movement were appropriate where would the poor average African woman get the funds to operate within this system? The logistics alone would defeat us. So let us turn to heavenly logistics!

SOCIAL INJUSTICE ACCORDING TO JESUS CHRIST

The Lord we serve is very sensitive to unhappy situations. He was and still is 'moved with compassion'. Thus he still desires to

a) Preach good news to the poor
b) Proclaim freedom for prisoners
c) Give recovery of sight to the blind
d) Release the oppressed
e) Proclaim the year of the Lord's favour (Lk. 4:18–19).

Before he left this world the Lord left us this work to continue. What are you and I doing about it? The social injustices of our present generation are abundant and they affect children and men as well as women. Some sufferers may have earned the problems they are grappling with but the Lord responded compassionately to people like this. So must we.

POST-PACWA INVOLVEMENT

Let us examine possible v'1ys in which we can be involved in procuring release for the oppressed, freedom for the prisoner etc. To prepare our minds for the task the following passages of scripture will help us–

Jeremiah 9:24; 22:15–16
Matthew 25:31–46
James 2:15–16

Let this conference be the end of your time of isolation from human problems. Act now! No longer say,

They are pretenders,
Their problems are self-made,
There is nothing that I can do,
I have my own problems and need help.

All these may very well be true but do not allow them to hinder you in your work for the kingdom. You can join an existing group of people or start a fresh one yourself to help–

1) Prisoners, both men and women
2) Hospital patients, especially those suffering from chronic conditions like TB, cancer, paralysis
3) Orphans
4) Abused women
5) Abused children
6) People in troubled marriages
7) Psychotic persons
8) Social outcastes (undefinable misfits, etc.)
9) Refugees

10) Bereaved individuals or families (widows, orphans etc.)
11) Beggars

Most of these areas are difficult to enter so do not step forward in your own strength or wisdom. Ask the Lord to show you the right area, to equip you and energize you. He will, he always does!

May the Lord keep us faithful till he comes again!

10

Battered Women

ROSEMARY MUMBI

DEFINITION

What is to batter? or battering? According to the English Language Dictionary – Collins Version: To batter some one, especially a child or a woman, means to injure them by hitting them many times, such as hitting with fists in order to knock the victim down. The supplementary explanation is that this hitting is done with great force driven by anger. That is the physical part. The emotional part is the mental torture and abuse that goes with battering. A battered woman is treated with contempt by her oppressor who is usually a husband or partner or cohabiter in the modern life in our cities. The battered victim is usually dependent, both materially and emotionally, upon her oppressor who may well be the man she loves and without whom her world would fall apart. Let's take a look at the kind of man who resorts to battering.

CULTURAL TRAITS

All over the world men have traditionally owned women and children for centuries. They have enjoyed the legal licence to use violence against women and children. The marriage licence, was a licence to hitting. In my own tribe BEMBA the morning after the wedding day is devoted to a ceremony called 'MASHIKULO'. It is a time for public advice from both families. It is not unusual for the father of the bride to advise the bridegroom 'not to spare the rod' should his wife become slightly disobedient. In the middle-East a Turkish Judge recently threw out a divorce request from a battered woman saying, 'A woman should not be left without a stick on her back nor food in her stomach' (No. 178 Sept. 1988 New International). In Britain wife battering became a crime only 26 years ago.

It is believed that in most of the Western world wife battering is now illegal. This statement does not tell us that it has diminished.

PSYCHOLOGICAL TRAITS

Some violent men are themselves the product of a violent upbringing. People like this have their own justifications for violence. They may say, 'If my parents had not beaten me I would have never made it in the world.' To them violence is a way of life. They would not hesitate to use it. Until the power of God convicts them, they would have no guilty feelings about it. Unfortunately for us, there are many people that go along with this kind of thinking.

ECONOMIC REASONS FOR VIOLENCE

Power is often associated with riches, the ability to possess a lot of money and property. Sometimes, owing to adverse economic conditions, husbands are unable to provide for their families. Such inability to be the breadwinner strikes a blow at the masculine ego. Many men feel devastated and confused. A man like this resorts to violence in order to hide his own feelings of inaequacy and insecurity.

This sense of insecurity is also evidenced in men who are emotionally illiterate. Such men are not sure of themselves; they can not stand up to aggression from other males because of their inferiority complexes. A man with an inferiority complex tends to project his frustrations and aggression on a victim who is less likely to pose any threat. Invariably such victims are women and children.

WRONGLY PROJECTED ANGER

Some men grow up with anti-social behaviour patterns because of bottled up anger that stems from their infancy. Some parents beat their infants and never give the children any reason for such punishment. For example, a cruel mother may raise a son who later grows up to be a woman hater; the kind that beats, murders or rapes women.

In conclusion, a battered woman is truly a broken woman mentally, physically and emotionally. She is a challenge to you and to me, to all of us Christian women.

WHERE TO BEGIN BUILDING

I would like to suggest a few challenges to all of us women of God, challenges designed to help to mend broken relationships in homes in order to help the *whole* families, husbands, wives and children in homes where battering occurs.

Creation of Awareness:

Creation of awareness in our local churches is step number one. Pray that the Lord will open your ears and eyes to be able to identify these needs around you. Even among 'Christians' there could be some that beat their wives.

To help a husband, do solicit the aid of the church elders whom he knows and *trusts*, or his own friends so that they can bring him to God. If he batters from economic reasons the church should help him to establish himself by leading him to identify his talents, skills, education and how he can best use them. But above all, befriend him in his need. He needs something in life – something to give him self-worth. The Bible tells us, 'Don't shut your heart or hand against the poor, lend them as much as they need' (Deut. 14:4–11).

Remember that men who batter are mostly insecure. They are bound to mistrust any offer of help. For this reason pray that the Lord will give you wisdom to lead him to God's security; pray that you will wear Christ's humility as you minister to him. People resent being 'put down' so seek to build them up. Your purpose is to mend, to restore people and to solve the problem by attacking the source of the trouble . . . the insecure man.

Is the woman innocent? She may be wrong but she is at the receiving end so are the children. The approach would be the same as to a man. Offer help with genuine humility. Let her *talk* about her problems mainly to let off steam. This will help release her bottled-up anger and bitterness.

PHYSICAL VIOLENCE

Physical violence can also come out of compulsive masculinity that drives boys and men to *love* violence as 'fun' or 'action'. For love of this 'action' many men join the Armed Forces, Streetgangs, Cults such as the Klu Klux Clan. In Zambia we have 'By Air Militants', political hooligans. Men join all these in order to express their virility. Basically men who are emotionally illiterate, are unable to express their feelings in a rational manner and tend to use the only language that will give them a feeling of superiority over their victim, i.e. physical violence.

WHAT ARE THE CONSEQUENCES OF BATTERING ON THE VICTIM?

There is physical pain to begin with. There is fear because the victim has no idea as to the extent of the physical damage.

But even worse is the emotional pain of being humiliated and degraded especially when such hitting is often followed by abusive lanaguage.

Being a battered woman leads to embarrassement and a deep sense of shame as the woman feels a total failure with regard to her marriage. She is likely to internalize her anger and not hit back. Her sense of shame is accentuated by the cultural belief that she is a 'bad' woman and that is why she is beaten. In other words society condemns her rather than her oppressor. Most often she is anxious to hide her hurt feelings. Sooner or later she starts to feel confused and guilty, believing that she is in the wrong or that she must have something in her that provokes the man's anger. She feels that she has failed in marriage and this feeling begins to erode her self confidence; because marriage is, in the African culture, an important measure of a woman's success.

As soon as her self-esteem begins to be eroded she begins to separate herself from her friends whom she fears might discover her unhappiness. She fears that they may hurt her already devastated self. She is so exasperated that she prefers to be alone with her misery; she withdraws into herself.

Walking around with bottled up anger and bitterness is very dangerous because it eventually produces an unhealthy and unbalanced personality.

Ask what in her opinion is the source of the trouble and don't pretend to know the solutions or simplify the solution with 'Try and keep happy because God will solve all your problems'. This is true but very hard for some one who is depressed. A more practical approach is to be preferred. Remember you have *no* power to change the situation. Try therefore to lead the person to start building their sense of worth by accepting that each person is God's gift to him/herself first and then to others. God loves this particular woman and longs to dwell in her as his very own Temple (Col. 3:12–15). God has a purpose for her life. God wants her to work very hard to use her hands to earn a living (1 Cor. 4:12; Th. 4:11; 2 Th. 3:10; 1 Th. 5:12; Col. 3:23).

In all these Bible readings God is telling us the importance of building our self-worth by using our hands and our talents in order to be economically self sufficient. When a woman is busy earning a living three things happen:–

The first is that she will be able to feed and clothe her household because she can afford it.

She will win love and respect from her husband. (Prov. 31:10–31) She has a sense of her self-esteem and she is living a full contented life in her Lord and Master through obeying him. In my opinion there would be no need to be a battered wife in normal circumstances.

TRAINING

The challenge for Christians is that there should be *training* in our local churches for counselling, facilitated perhaps by PACWA. I would like to suggest ten women from each Country to undergo such training so that they can create a pool of resource people in every nation. Such a pool of resource people should conduct counselling sessions in all churches regardless of denomination. We need to spread this knowledge in every corner of Africa.

Finally it is time we established Skills Training Centres for women for the purpose of *developing* them fully. Such centres should be designed both to build character and to develop talents for any girl or woman. An integral part of any such programme should be an income generating component. Battered women are broken women. Let us lend a hand to build them up.

But let us be careful, as we help a family to be economically sound. Our final objective should be to BUILD A FAMILY, A WHOLE FAMILY FOR GOD. A FAMILY IN WHICH THERE IS A STRONG RELATIONSHIP WITH GOD. A FAMILY THAT GIVES PROMINENCE TO JESUS AS RULER AND KING OF THEIR LIVES . . . THIS IS THE ONLY EXPERIENCE THAT WILL PRODUCE A 'WHOLESOME FAMILY LIFE'.

11

Child Abuse in Africa

F. N. CHOLA

Child abuse is a wide and complicated subject. In the time allocated to this paper, it will not be possible to discuss the subject in much detail. I shall present a brief outline of the subject and also raise questions for discussions.

In trying to solve the problems of child abuse, it is necessary to realize that it is a problem that is more widespread and has increased more in urban areas than in rural areas. In urban areas, cultural values are ignored or even inverted, and the result is a situation where children are no longer supported by the neighbourhood society, nor arc instances of manifest child abuse, rebuked or regarded as socially unacceptable as they would often be in a rural setting. So our urban societies are a fertile ground for cases of child abuse. What can be done to help protect the child from such situations?

CHILD NEGLECT

Child neglect is a form of child abuse and can be split into two categories. A child who is deprived of a parent or guardian by death, illness or abandonment, often finds himself neglected, especially in the urban community. The other category is when parents are alive and present, but are making no effort to maintain their child. Instances of child neglect and abuse may occur in the following circumstances.

1. Single mothers unable to care for their children.
2. Families where one parent has been deserted or where there has been a divorce.
3. Families where children are delinquent and disobedient.
4. Families where a parent or parents are imprisoned.
5. Families where a parent, especially a mother, has become a psychiatric case due to social or other problems.
6. Polygamous marriages where there is ill-feeling between the wives.

71

CHILD ABUSE

This refers to ill treatment and encouragement of bad habits. It takes on two major forms.

(a) Physical abuse which is easily detected.
(b) Mental or Psychological Abuse, which is more difficult to identify in early stages.

This often becomes apparent afterwards. It often consists of the withholding of affection, from rejection and *in extreme* cases, the enslavement of a child. It is often discovered through the effects of neglect and the incidental ill-treatment which often accompanies it.

CULTURAL/SOCIAL CONFLICTS

The urbanization of our societies has brought about various problems. The vacuum left by the absence of the extended communal responsibility for the welfare of the child has resulted in neglect, abuse and resultant delinquency. The grandmother figure who taught young girls about life; the one a girl went to when she had a problem is now missing. Now we have cases of girls burning themselves or committing suicide because there is no one on whom to off-load their anxieties. Who will teach our young men and women to be responsible citizens and how is that going to be done? I am asking these questions so that I can stimulate your thoughts on these issues.

SEXUAL EXPLOITATION:

There has been an increase in cases of sexual abuse. Young girls are becoming pregnant at very tender ages. Who is responsible? Who is to blame? Fathers are sleeping with their own daughters. What's causing this cancer? How do we prevent it and protect the poor child. (e.g. father says 'I am teaching you'.) There is the ever present problem of sugar daddies ruining young girls. Parents are encouraging their children to become prostitutes to support themselves. (e.g. father tells daughter to provide for the home through prostitution.) Parents are performing or causing abortions to be performed on their daughters, making them barren by destroying their reproductive systems or even killing their daugher in the process, due to infections etc. Just imagine the effect sex abuse will have on the child.

CHILD BATTERING

There are cases of step-parents and occasional cases of a natural parent killing a child through excessive beating, starvation etc. There are cases of extreme mental torture that have psychiatric effects on children. Children are maimed for life.

DIVORCE

What is its effect on the child? If parents re-marry shouldn't children be consulted? Who should the child live with? What if the stepmother does not want her and the real mother is too busy amusing her new husband? You can imagine what such a child goes through. She/he may end up homeless. What is the treatment accorded to the child? What happens to children born outside marriage where husbands insist that these should be kept in their houses with the other kids? There are children whose physical needs are met but who receive no love.

CHILDREN IN PRISONS/PARENTS IN PRISONS

Some children have gone to prison with their parents. Is this legal? What treatment do they receive? What happens to those children left at home when a bread-winner is imprisoned?

CHILD LABOUR

What is the traditional set-up in relationship to the urban set up? What about children who work for their education; children who work to support their families; children who work to survive; the street child who is tough and suspicious? How do we handle such children in order to win their confidence and be able to help them? Where do we find the trained personnel to handle them? In most African countries, there is a shortage of trained Social Workers. How do we organize the street children in groups of productive units. Is the whole concept of child labour evil? If not where and when does it become a problem?

THE CHILD'S HEALTH

Health facilities in most African countries leave much to be desired. How do we improve a child's health under the present economic situations? Children have died from lack of adequate medical care. What is our solution to this problem? What do we do about the increase in malnutrition cases which is fast becoming one of the worst killers of children? Recurring cases may be due to abuse or neglect.

PLACES OF SAFETY, REFORMATORIES AND APPROVED SCHOOLS

What facilities exist in these institutions? Are they serving the purpose for which they were formed? What can we do to ensure the child's interest is protected in these institutions?

VOLUNTARY HOMES:

Are these supervised according to the law? Who should ensure that these children's right are protected? If children are abused, how should the homes be closed without endangering the well-being of the children?

COURTS OF LAW

I have been to courts where juveniles cases are handled in open court. How do we ensure that the Law is followed? What should happen to the juvenile at the time of arrest? Remand prisons are not separate from adult remand facilities. What should be done? How do the police handle juveniles? Our present legal system leaves much to be desired, where juvenile cases are concerned. What should be the role of the Social Services Department?

There are many questions and situations we can discuss today. We won't have the time. What is important is that to find solutions to child abuse and neglect and their implications is a common duty. The Church, the family, civic officers, educators, N.G.O.s., houses, Governments have all a role to play in the prevention of child abuse and protection of the child.

CONCLUSION:

Cases of child abuse have such a harming effect on the child that we need to examine seriously ways of improving the situation. Divorce should be avoided as much as possible especially where there are children. The church and society as a whole has to work out a support system for abused children who may need counselling and rehabilitation.

Our Governments need to budget more money for the development of the child. The child should enjoy special protection and should be given opportunities, and facilities to enable him/her to develop physically, mentally, morally, spiritually and socially, in a healthy and normal manner. Unless this is done, governments will find themselves spending more money on correctional institutions e.g. reformatories.

Unless we put God first in our children's lives and show them God's love, both in action and words, we shall be partly responsible for these lost souls. The church has to come alive and play a more active role in the protection of the child and in preventing child abuse. The church can contribute more towards raising the public consciousness regarding child abuse.

12

AIDS – A Challenge to the Church

EVA SANDERSON

AIDS has become a household name in the world today. It is a subject for many conversations, on the streets, behind closed doors, in seminars and conferences.

The Media carries information and warns the public against this deadly disease. Almost every one has some mental picture of AIDS. For some, when they hear the word AIDS they see hopelessness and doom. Others see suffering and death. What is your picture of AIDS? What is this AIDS?

ACQUIRED   – Transmitted from an infected person to another person.
IMMUNE   – The body's immune system is impaired or damaged by the virus.
DEFICIENCY – T4 Lymphocytes are damaged, reduced in numbers or deficient.
SYNDROME   – Consists of a cluster of clinical features which demonstrate impairment of the bodies' defence system. i.e.

1. Persistent fever and night sweats
2. Swollen (lymph) glands in the neck, armpits and groin
3. Marked tiredness and fatigue
4. Weight loss
5. Diarrhoea

Some other symptoms may appear such as spots on the tongue, headaches, visual problems, skin rashes, bleeding and bruising.

AIDS was first identified in the United States in 1979 in members of the homosexual community. It has now been reported in many countries of the world including Africa. It is thought to be more widely spread in some countries in Africa than others.

The cause of AIDS is a virus of which two variants have so far been identified. The virus is capable of mutation like the influenza virus. This causes problems for the finding of cures and the development of vaccines. In the western world, the main groups at present who are at risk are male homosexuals and intravenous drug users.

Evidently in Africa the spread of the virus is mainly among the sexually active heterosexuals.

Infection with the AIDS virus is likely to continue spreading rapidly unless sexual behaviour alters.

A successful vaccine or cure will not be available for some years to come, if at all.

The condition is ultimately diagnosed by laboratory tests including a blood test which detects the presence of the virus.

When AIDS was first discovered reactions from various national leaders and the general populace varied immensely. Some were more interested to know where it came from and who brought it. Some denied that it was new and asked why the fuss. Others denied its existence to avoid panic and loss of business, especially tourism. To admit they had a disaster on their hands meant taking action to avert it.

Some Christians rejoiced; they saw AIDS as judgement upon our godless decadent society and hoped that through it many people would turn to God. They saw AIDS as capable of visiting only the non christians – the world out there. Christ's command to his disciples was for them to go out into the world and make disciples. Our churches are full of women whose husbands are not Christians and do not believe they need to live by biblical principles. These plus the fact that AIDS is also spread through the mother to the unborn baby and through blood transfusions, has brought the problem into the church while making it a problem of the church.

AIDS is a challenge to the church. No purpose can be served by recriminations against any section of the population held to be responsible. Instead we should offer to sufferers, unconditional and practical compassion. It would be unfortunate too if reaction took the form of a merciless and self-righteous moral backlash. Something much more radical and constructive is called for than the scourging of the other people's vices. If this catastrophe is to be averted, there must be an urgent and immediate reappraisal of our attitudes and behaviour in matters of sexual conduct and human relationships.

EDUCATION

AIDS – Is there hope? Will knowledge save us? Preaching isn't going to save us either – even good preaching. Most parents have preached the right gospel to their children on matters of sexuality even if they have not preached what they have practised themselves.

The grim statistics of teenage pregnancy, abortion and sexually transmitted diseases bear testimony. The best preachers in the world can't keep teenagers out of trouble for ever. When they leave the church, the voice and words of the preacher meet with competition from other voices telling the teenagers what to do.

Knowledge has not stopped the spread of sexually transmitted diseases. Knowledge of the use of contraceptives has not cut down the pregnancy rate; it has increased it. With no vaccine and no cure in sight, education is our only hope.

There are two kinds of education on AIDS:–

a) CHASTITY – This is moral, it is traditional and it works.
b) 'SAFE SEX' – It professes to be moral, it is liberal and it does not work.

Chastity is the traditional Judeo-Christian view. This is by and large practised by most African tribes.

The more liberal, educated, tolerant and progressive people know better. They believe that sex is lots of fun and if something is fun then it must be healthy, so they forget about chastity and get on with fornication and how healthy have they (and we) been?

Yet the only thing that could have prevented all this pain, sorrow, sickness and decay of society was a traditional practice of chastity.

AIDS therefore has given the church an opportunity to restate and emphasize the biblical guide-line for living.

It should speak clearly and boldly on questions of moral and sexual ethics, using every means possible to teach in schools, on radio, T.V. and in newspapers.

The church must be conversant with the latest information on the disease in order to spread knowledge not panic. It should take a leading role in the AIDS crisis and work with other interested organizations.

In order to educate people on how to curb the spread of AIDS, the church must live what it preaches; chastity before marriage and fidelity in marriage. It must remind the people of God's warning against ungodliness and sin (Rom. 1; Exod. 15:26).

These high ideals can be reached through:–

– Marriage enrichment programmes for married couples
– Marriage Seminars for the unmarried, which should include choosing the right partner and the fact that having sex is not part of courtship.
– Challenging and training parents to understand and feel comfortable with their sexuality, so that they can teach family life education and sex education to others including their children.
– Adequate pre-marriage counselling to young people.
– Church youth activities should include discussions and debate on AIDS.
– Adequate information and literature should be made available to those who may in turn want to teach other groups.

Christians should be well informed about the population policies adopted in their countries and the methods employed to that end. Some countries allow contraceptives to teenagers without the knowledge and consent of parents. This tells the children that sex is all right provided you do not get pregnant. When contraception fails, abortion is easily offered. Contraception and abortion may prevent birth but they will not prevent AIDS. This practice also has another serious consequence; it encourages promiscuity. The church should also understand and pass on the fact that birth control pills weaken resistance to infection, further increasing susceptibility to AIDS. The church does not have to buy the merchandise pedalled by the population experts. The church has not been called to conform to this age but to transform it (Rom. 12:2).

In most African traditions when a married person dies a near kinsman or kinswoman is given to succeed the deceased in the marriage. This is presently one way in which AIDS is being spread. The church should take a stand and discourage the practice where the cause of death is known or suspected to be AIDS.

The church should provide counselling services and facilitate open sharing to break the news when one of the spouses is found to be HIV positive. It should also encourage the couple to avoid infecting each other. This may include advising the afflicted partner to offer not to have sex for the rest of his or her life. It would be a sacrifice of love. It is not impossible. Every human being is capable of that sacrifice through God.

THE AIDS VICTIM

AIDS seems to be affecting mainly the most productive and sexually active members of the population, those in the 17–50 age group. This group includes most bread winners. Therefore AIDS does not affect only the individual, it affects partners, families, communities and nations.

The implications of being pronounced HIV positive are many, such as:

a) Prolonged illness from any opportunistic diseases.
b) Rejection, stigmatization and alienation.
c) Prospect of having to break the news to their families and friend.
d) Fear of infecting others, and the knowledge that they may already have done so.
e) Loss of prospects for safe marriage and having children.
f) Death.

People who have their immune systems damaged by HIV are particularly vulnerable to infection. They will have varying degrees of illness and a wide variety of symptoms. Some will become physically weak and emaciated some will become blind, some incontinent and other will show signs of brain damage.

Although many will receive care from hospitals, most of the care and support will be personal from families, friends, neighbours and the church. These will give the basic home-care – washing, feeding, changing and offering comfort.

AIDS should be seen as a human disease like any other. The victims should be treated with the same care and compassion as people suffering from any other disease. The teaching and example of Jesus Christ must be followed (Matt. 25:35–36; 1 Tim. 5:10). We cannot make any distinction here on the grounds of the nature of the disease or the manner in which it is contracted.

We are called to bear one another's burdens and with God's perfect love working in us, fear will be cast out, giving us greater freedom to serve the needy.

The church has a counselling role to play in preparing victims to accept their condition and to facilitate breaking the news to the spouses. For some it may include challenging them and encouraging them to change their life styles. For those who are not Christians, an invitation for them to meet Christ and make him Lord and Saviour of their lives should be given.

Relatives and the victims need encouragement, hope, friendship, compassion, care and support.

There needs to be a genuine sense of intimacy, of sharing another's burdens of fear, anger and anxiety. This will alleviate suffering and bring comfort.

During the prolonged illness of the AIDS victim those closest to the family are involved in front line care. The church should help in this area if possible. There are however many other areas of need, such as: cleaning of the patient's house and giving personal care, perhaps shopping, taking care of children, providing transport to and from schools, offering hospitality to someone nursing a loved one far away from home and offering financial help.

The church should promote home and community care through Christian communities. In some areas there is need to build hospices so as to alleviate congestion in government hospitals and give specialized care.

WIDOWS AND ORPHANS

God has made provision in his Word for them.

a) They are to be defended (Ps. 68:5; Is. 1:17; Jer. 22:3).
b) Their needs are to be given proper recognition (1 Tim. 5:3; Acts 6:1).
c) They are to be supported (Deut. 24:17).
d) They are to be looked after (Jas. 1:27).
e) Their assets are to be protected (Prov. 23:10).

Most of our people do not write or leave wills. The result is that their assets are liable to be plundered by relatives, leaving widows and orphans destitute.

The church should teach the importance of leaving a will and honouring it. The church should be represented during funerals to protect the bereaved and their property.

CARE OF ORPHANS

AIDS by its nature of commonly taking both parents through death is leaving behind many orphans. Traditionally African families have, through the extended family system, always been able to take care of their orphans. However, the recent fast move from the extended family to the nuclear family system, compounded by AIDS, calls for new solutions. To this end Christians with smaller or grown up families and those with no children may want to consider fostering or adopting these children. Interest and intention declared before the death of parents will enable future adoptive parents to share in the parents' suffering, their care and grief. The process will comfort the dying parents and ease the transition for the children.

The church may wish to give a subsidy to families who adopt the children.

THE ELDERLY

AIDS in addition to leaving behind many orphans is taking away the comfort of the older generation – their children. Many old parents and grandparents will be left without hope and care. This is yet another challenge for the church. The church will have to evaluate its programmes and activities in order to provide for this category of the needy.

POST PACWA

United in the love of Christ and concerned for the souls, bodies and minds of our society Pan African Christian women should join together so that Christian resources are released to serve the people in need. They should be knowledgeable about AIDS and make sure that members of their committee are informed.

They should be willing to act as resource people in churches, communities, schools etc.

- Be involved in youth projects.
- Offer guidance on sexual behaviour and relationships.
- Take a stand on the promotion of condoms for 'safer sex'.
- Assume a higher profile in the pastoral and counselling areas of care.
- Actively plan to influence public opinion as much and as quickly as possible to change the commonly accepted view that courting and dating include sexual intercourse.
- Constantly remind society of the importance of chastity before marriage and fidelity in marriage.
- Promote youth work:
  a. Youth clubs for enjoyment and opportunities for personal growth;
  b. Unemployed youth – cash generating projects;
  c. Undertake project to prevent prostitution and to rehabilitate prostitutes;
- Evaluate the need in your area and consider the possibility of a hospice.

HELP community to prepare for a caring role by facilitating seminars on 'Basic Nursing Skills'.

- Pray for your Country, for Africa and the World:
a. For change of attitudes and life styles;
b. For success of research being undertaken;
c. For Governments charged with responsibility and leadership of the nations;
d. For the church to grow in wisdom, boldness, compassion and love.

13

The Sorcerer and Pagan Practices

MADAME NANAN

SORCERY AND THE SORCERER

It is easier to describe the practice of sorcery than actually to define what sorcery is. There are various titles which are given to a sorcerer: magician, fetisher, healer. All these titles may describe the same man and there is no distinction between them.

We can, however, say that sorcery is a group of evil practices carried out by a sorceror. It is a fact that he possesses the power to do evil. He uses his powers to hurt, destroy and kill. In general we can say that a sorcerer uses his powers to do evil and not to do good.

Magic is one of the means employed by a sorcerer. It can be used in the service of religion. We can find an example of this in the times of the Pharaohs of Egypt and also in the east. Such magic is used for both good and evil purposes.

Fetishes are objects made or changed to which is attributed an occult force for the purposes either of defence or aggression, of good or evil. Examples of these are statues of one's ancestors or of animals.

Another instrument of the sorcerer is that of the curse. His word is a powerful weapon and can be used to bring death upon another person.

The Bible itself illustrates the power of the word. It was by his word that God created the world and it was by their spoken words that Jesus and his followers performed miracles.

By one's word one can bless or curse. The sorcerer is very much aware of this. We who are involved in the ministry of evangelization know that one of our weapons is the Word of God (Eph. 6:14, 17).

Witchcraft and the Spell

This activity involves the use of a substitute for the person involved. An image may be made, or an object such as a lock of hair or something else connected with the person may be used. The wounds inflicted upon the image are supposed to be transferred to the person concerned.

A spell consists of the infliction by means of charms or magical rites of a change in the physical or mental health of the person for whom the sorcerer intends such a change.

One sorcerer who was later converted spoke in his testimony of the fact that he was able to put a spell on a whole village by placing a talisman at the source of their supply of drinking water. By doing this he turned the hearts of the people against the Word of God.

A sorcerer may enlist the use of a thunderbolt against a thief in order to reclaim what has been stolen.

Among the people of the Oubangui (Central Africa) the sorcerer makes use of a metal dart. This is impregnated with poison from various plants. He then speaks to the dart, telling it to carry out its mission and then to return to him within three days. The dart is moved by a mysterious power, then with a sound like a roll of thunder it flies off and disappears, leaving behind it a luminous trail. It hovers over the roof of its victim's house to watch for the appearance of the object of its spite and then it returns.

Such spells are considered to be the source of failure, misfortune and illness and they cause much tension in local communities.

Metamorphosis into Animals

This is not just an illusion but the facts force one to the belief that it actually takes place.

One sorcerer who was later converted witnessed to the fact that he could turn himself into a snake. His bite had brought death to those attacked by him. He had also changed himself into a dog and a goat to stray across a road and cause an accident. The same brother recounted how he had been given the task of dispersing a conference of the Assemblies of God. He arrived at the place where it was being held. But there he met a dense cloud. He could not approach because an army with fiery swords guarded the place. He decided to transform himself into a snake to harm the evangelist and the church leaders. But he was unable to do so. All were protected by the angel host. They could say like the psalmist: 'In God I put my trust. I will not fear. What can men do unto me?' (Ps. 56:1–2).

Indeed the sorcerer cannot be assured of success when he tries to hurt someone. One such man attempted to harm my father. He had developed the practice of placing images of his victims in a pan of boiling water. Nobody expect for my father escaped death by this means. But when the sorcerer plunged the image of my father into the boiling water, the pan broke into small pieces. He repeated the experiment and on the third occasion used a cast-iron pan. But he was still not successful. By now he had realized that there was a power greater than his own. My father said simply that his power was guaranteed by the one in whom he placed his trust – the all-powerful God.

BELIEF IN SPIRITS

People believe in many kinds of spirit forces. They control culture, people's homes, professions and social classes.

The spirits of the earth are the authors of disease such as measles and smallpox. Rituals are needed to ward off such diseases.

Other spirits send the rain. There are those who bring good fishing to those who work at sea. Such spirits require blood sacrifices and especially human sacrifices.

Sometimes these spirits are thought of as if they were like human beings. It is possible to deceive them.

In thinking about these inumerable spirits or lesser deities one can observe a certain dualism which describes black gods and white gods. The black gods are the gods of evil, the white of good. Over these lesser gods is the chief god and here too we have the good and the evil god.

PAGAN PRACTICES

To understand the practices of the pagan one must first understand his view of life.

All life is seen as coming from one source and is lived according to a predetermined plan. Life goes on beyond the grave so that 'Those who are dead are not dead'. They live in the home of the dead. This explains the cult of and prayers to the dead persons. The dead are invoked in order to keep in touch with the source of one's own life.

Certain tenets are held to firmly by the people:

1. a belief in unseen powers
2. a belief in God and his power
3. absolute obedience to God
4. repentance and reparation by means of animal sacrifices
5. belief in the immortality of the soul
6. belief in the power of the world.

To the African life itself is supremely precious and sacred. The murderer is to be put to death. Anyone who kills somebody else accidentally has to undertake special rites to avoid being disturbed by his victim.

The sacred character of human life calls for the observance of certain rules and practices in order to protect and prolong it.

The African's Perception of his Place in Creation and his Relationship to his Creator

Everything in creation is contained within a system. So the African has a sense of his relationship with all that surrounds him: the earth, the air, the sun, the rain, work, health, wealth, the working of the law, forbidden things, customs, traditions.

Between the African and God whom he describes as the 'Great God', there is a multitude of intermediaries. These range from universal and local spirits, oracles and priests down to the ordinary, powerless people.

Everything which comes into the world is a reincarnation of what has been before with its own archytypal character or *kpoli*. One needs, therefore, to know one's origins and what is forbidden to one to live according to one's own archetypal character.

To become a 'man' in the African sense of the word one must cross the different orders of age by means of initiation ceremonies. One must obtain the power or commit oneself to the powers of invisible spirits. These are known as the power of clairvoyance, of divination, of the oracle, of the ordeal etc.

Clairvoyance: This is the gift of understanding the past, the present and the future. The clairvoyant has the power to see what is hidden from most people.

Divination: This is the power to see the future by using occult instruments such as the oracle or astrology. Astrology is a method which has been brought into the country from abroad and interests many modern Africans.

Oracle: The oracle receives from a god or a spirit the answer to his questions.

Ordeal: This is a form of judgment from God brought through the spirits. One submits to the ordeal in order to prove one's innocence. This may be through poison or by fire or by some other means. The practice of the ordeal is very common in all regions.

The Power of the Blessing

There are three kinds of blessing.

1. The blessing of favour. Here the donor expresses a wish for the good fortune of the devotee who benefits from the sympathy and goodwill of the spiritual leader. From the Bible one has the example of the blessing which Jacob stole from his brother.

2. Blessing brought by power. Prayer is offered to the invisible powers on behalf of someone.

3. Blessing commanded on someone. Here good things or power is passed directly from the donor to the one who is being blessed. The blessing is received without the intervention of any rituals.

The Gikuyus

Here, as in most of Africa there is belief in one supreme God who dwells in heaven. He has a secondary home in the heights of the mountains. In the case of the Gikuyus the official earthly home of the *Ngai* or 'Lord of Brightness' is the summit of mount Kenya. This great God has little interest in the human race except at the four great moments in life: birth, initiation, grave illness and death.

Anyone who wishes for help from *Ngai* can approach him only through the intermediary of the family group. We can recall the words of Jesus that where two or three are gathered in his name he is there in the midst of them.

Initiation Ceremonies

The Kabye live in north Togo. They are organized according to age-groupings. At the age of 13 the boys are separated and live in a separate commune in a state of partial autonomy. There are two sets of initiation ceremonies, at the age sof 21 and 25. After the ceremony has been completed the men are free to marry.

The girls undergo their initiation ceremonies at the age of 16.

Marriage

At the end of the initiation ceremonies the maternal uncle of the man exhorts him to find a fiancée. The initiation of the female is the prelude to her marriage. She will receive a staff sent by her fiancé which is a token of their engagement. Up to the time of her initiation the future bridegroom will work in the field of his father-in-law and give presents to her family. After her initiation the young woman will confirm the choice which her parents have made by accepting the staff. A few months before the marriage the young woman will move to the house of her in-laws. She will cease to be a girl and will be married in the house of her 'husband'. It is a marriage with a dowry.

Death

In African society death is always regarded as something bad. It forms an occasion for the manifestation of both community and family solidarity so that all one's friends come to support the family in its mourning.

Laments, tears and gifts (in cash or in kind) are signs of participation in the grief of the family.

It is an occasion for calling upon one's ancestors. Such consultations lead to knowledge of the cause of death. The dead are called upon to avenge themselves and not to rest idly in the abode of the dead.

After the death has taken place of a husband or wife the widow or widower has to submit to certain ceremonies.

The ceremonies are more rigid for a widow than for a widower. The period of widowhood varies from one to four months for the man and from four to twelve months for the woman.

In most cases the widow has to seek for a new husband within the family of her former husband. The man, on the other hand, can choose a new wife where he will.

CONCLUSIONS

These are the main ideas which are at the heart of African practice. If we study these beliefs carefully we see that they are not bad in themselves. On the contrary they are of value if we seek to live our lives in the light of the gospel. Thus, to live with African values but also in the light of the gospel can make of us fine Christians.

Let us consider again those African values which are not bad in themselves.

A true African has an unshakeable belief in his God.
He is always faithful to his god.
He seeks to live in a right relationship to the world which surrounds him and to the unseen spirits.
He gives great importance to the life of the community.

He realizes the need for a mediator between himself and the God who is most powerful and most holy.

He considers that life itself has a supreme value and that nothing else is as important.

He believes that everyone has a true calling in life to which they should apply themselves.

He welcomes the new-born and seeks protection for them from his god against all that would harm them.

He makes arrangements for the upbringing and initiation of his children and seeks their welfare both before and during their marriage.

He knows that he lives constantly in the presence of his god.

He is faithful to him in all things and in all places and at all times.

He relies on the one whom he knows to be the source of his life. The African has a natural knowledge that it is wrong to steal and to commit adultery etc. and he seeks to punish those who sin.

He realizes the value of marriage and seeks to preserve this value by all means.

But however good may be these basic beliefs, the African must still realize that he needs the inspiration of the Holy Spirit to turn such beliefs into practical living. All the time that his beliefs are not enlightened by the Holy Spirit or when they are practised without the light of the gospel they remain contrary to the will of God.

The evidence of this lies in thse facts: The African does not believe that life is a divine reality which one receives from God, the one and only source through Jesus Christ. He thinks that life is a material reality which he receives from his ancestors.

Instead of worshipping God through Jesus Christ as the only Mediator the African worships creatures through which he thinks that God has given life to the world and for which reason he fears these creatures.

Instead of accepting the power of God which rules over the world, Satan, sin and death through Jesus Christ, the African seeks out spiritual powers such as fetishes to give him the power to live his life whereby Satan, sin and death becomes his absolute masters.

He does not have fellowship will the all-powerful God who is the source of wisdom and of all good. Rather, cut off from his true source of life he joins himself to lifeless things which are the works of his own hands. He struggles to maintain his life while at the same time he cuts himself off from his life's true source.

Instead of considering as members of his own family all those who receive their life from God he has concern only for those who share his ancestry and his blood.

The African thinks that he has been destined for reincarnation whereas God has planned that he should inherit eternal life.

Thus, it is not for us to reject automatically African values. Rather we should pray that God will enlighten us and direct us in the practice of these values. Truly throughout the world African beliefs are good and valuable. Evangelists should use them as the base of true evangelism.

In conclusion, those values which go to make up African culture have not been incorporated into our Christian practices even though we live as

Africans. Of course, to be African does not mean practising the occult or polygamy etc. It does mean to have such values as faithfulness to God, communication and a relationship with the unseen world, to live a harmonious community life, to bring to God our joys and sorrows.

Thus we can say that the African possesses those values which predispose him to be a good Christian. It is enough that he should be a good African and that he should be enlightened by the Holy Spirit so that that light transforms the values by which he lives. In so doing he will perfectly live out the gospel.

In a society dominated by the practices and beliefs of our ancestors and where the men and women in our churches are failing in one way or another we need to repent in order for our faith to advance.

May the Spirit of God guard us so that, purified by the blood of our glorious Saviour, we may be able to be powerful instruments in the hands of the one and only God, the Creator of the heavens and the earth, who in his great mercy has called us to his service.

.14

Sexual Abuse

MAUREEN MNKANDLA

Probably no group suffers more trauma than the sexually abused. Our time has come to uncover this hidden sin, sound an alarm for the church and our governments, offer hope and healing for the victims or survivors of sexual abuse. Many survivors of sexual abuse carry scars inflicted on them by the actions of others for the rest of their lives.

SEXUAL ABUSE DEFINED

Sexual abuse is any act involving sexual molestation and exploitation, including, but not limited to incest, rape and sodomy by one person on another.

Myths abound about sexual victimization. This ignorance serves as a foundation for legal and social practices offered in dealing with victims of sexual abuse.

For purposes of this seminar we will look primarily at child sexual abuse as most sexually abused women have also been sexually abused as children.

HISTORY OF SEXUAL ABUSE

Sexual abuse of children has existed throughout history and across cultures. Societal values of the particular period determine whether it is called abuse or not. There is usually a predominant attitude in any given society at any given period in history. Changes in thought about particular sexual practices have occurred in a cyclical rather than a linear fashion. What is normal today may be considered differently in another decade. Compare the attitude to bikini-bra dancers on beaches with those about a century ago to the skin covers of Africans. A behaviour pattern begins as normal, becomes immoral, then criminal, then psychopathological and perhaps reverts to normal. For instance, homosexuality was considered as normal in ancient Roman civilization. The Greeks regarded it as a superior form of sexuality. Currently, in most societies, it is regarded as a psychiatric disorder. For us as Christians the Bible remains our standard and for us the practice is immoral.

With the decline of the church as the prevailing authoritarian body in most of our countries the judicial systems have become the sanctioning body against sexual involvement with children, with the following being the charges normally filed:

- Indecent Act
- Indecent Assault
- Statutory Rape
- Sodomy
- Gross Indecency
- Incest
- Contributing to delinquency of a minor
- Exhibitionism
- Fondling

What charge is filed often depends on the evidence available and the likelihood of obtaining a conviction.

With the exception of a short period between 1650 and 1660 incest was not considered a criminal offence in England until 1908.

PRESENT SEXUAL ABUSE

All definitions are culture and time bound. Most legal and medical definitions fail to take into account the psychological and interactive aspects. Legislation and the law are not a panacea for all social problems but only a framework within which a particular problem may be addressed. The law will only punish and hopefully deter the perpetrator but does not extend services or offer treatment to the abused child or his family. Our time has come to do something about the victims or survivors of child abuse.

Sexually abused children continue to be abused by the system and a society unwilling to confront the problem. We see this in the lenient sentences often meted out to rapists and other sexual molestors or the society that takes reported cases too lightly or the therapist who proposes to take his patient into his bed in order to heal sexual hangups.

Those trying to fight sexual abuse often face other and sometimes more powerful opponents who believe that there is nothing harmful about child/adult sexual relationships. In the US for example some organized groups are lobbying to promote child-adult sexual relationships.
a) The North American Man/Boy Love Association (NAMBLA) urges that the age of consent should be lowered to 4 years.
b) The Rene Guyon Society in Southern California has a motto 'Sex before age 8 or else it's too late'.
c) The Childhood Sensuality Circle (CSC) in San Diego has a 9 point statement of purpose concerning the sexual rights of children.

So what has that got to do with us in Africa? As with most things today what is in the US today is here tomorrow. What are we as a church in Africa doing about it? These people in the US are lobbying for laws at State and federal level to be changed with regard to children and sex. We, the Christian women in Africa, may not be many in numbers but our time has come to rise up and be heard, promoting the child protection laws in the area of sexual abuse especially and lobbying for their introduction in those areas where they are non-existent. Let us become organized, vocal and powerful.

EFFECTS OF CHILD SEXUAL ABUSE

It is difficult to establish an absolute cause and effect relationship but research evidence suggests negative and damaging effects of sexual abuse with long-range effects on the quality of personal adjustments and interpersonal relationships. Most researchers do not even fully comprehend the total extent and frequency of abuse. The effects may vary in intensity and severity but they are common to most victims or survivors of sexual abuse.

They come under several headings.

The Physical Effects

– Feeding and sleeping disturbances in infants and toddlers
– Bed wetting in school age children
– Dysmenorrhea and amenorrhea in teenagers
– Vulvar lacerations and abrasions in the genital region
– STD's (VD, AIDS etc.)
– Pregnancy leading to abortion or unwanted pregnancies which can both be very traumatic for a teenager who is still a child herself.
– Possible cervical cancer. Early intercourse can be a predisposing factor in the incidence of cervical cancer.
– Obesity: There is some speculation that there may be a link between obesity and sexual abuse, especially incest.

Psychosomatic Effects

– migraines
– stomach and skin problems
– disabling aches and pains

Emotional Effects

Guilt: I must be evil or why did this happen to me?
　　　　Why did I receive its pleasurable stimulation?
　　　　Why have I taken my mother's sexual partner? (in incest cases)
　　　　Why did I hide the truth? (where there are threats and bribes)
This raises the question of why victims do not tell.

a) They feel loyalty and love towards the abuser.
b) When they talk about it they are not believed.
c) Often they are told by the abuser who is in authority over them that the act is acceptable but must be kept a secret.
d) There are real or implied threats.
e) Nobody asks.

Shame

They feel dirty and worthless.
They suffer from a lack of self-esteem.
In adulthood they let others take advantage of them.

Anger and hatred

This often leads to depression which in turn leads to suicide where the anger turns inward or to irrational fury often directed against children or husband where the anger turns outward. It is an energy-consuming anger.

Fear and unfocused anxiety

They are afraid to show affection to their family and friends.
They fear that their husbands may interfere with their children.
    These fears may eventually fragment the marriage.

Behavioural Effects

– Negative and self-destructive behaviour patterns such as seeking escape through alcohol and drug abuse
– Running away, often leading to prostitution
– Promiscuity as a form of self-punishment or as an attempt to achieve a measure of control by repetition of the act. Whatever the dynamics of promiscuity in the case of most survivors of sexual abuse it is a cry for love and affection. Having received confusing signals about how love is given and expressed by adults whom they trusted, these teenagers lack the ability to distinguish between genuine caring and casual sex.

Relational Effects

Marriage

– lack of trust in men
– ambivalent feelings ranging from aversion to addiction to the sexual act
– sexual problems, including vaginismus
– flashback memories

Lesbianism

– It feels like a safer sexual attachment. This has not been adequately researched but many survivors tell of homosexual experiences in their search for love.

Parenting

– The survivor constantly has to fight two tendencies.
    a) repeating abusive behaviour patterns
    b) Overprotectedness. There is mistrust of any adults near their children and even suspicion of their own husbands. When it comes to parenting the

survivor of child sexual abuse is working from poor models where the crime was perpetrated by one of their parents or where their parents colluded in the act.

INCEST

This crosses class barriers. It is permitted or tolerated in certain cultures such as that of black Zimbabwe. My paternal aunt's husband can impose sexual demands on me.

It is likely to arise in stress situations such as where the father is jobless and spends the day at home drinking etc.

It may arise when the offender suffers from mental subnormality or a personality disorder.

It may arise under constitutions of marital discord with sexual estrangement.

There is also 'Nganga' (witchdoctor) incited incest.

It arises in all relationships – father/daughter; mother/son; father/son; mother/daughter. There are also cases of multiple incest.

RAPE

This is largely a product of youth and a desire to exhibit masculinity. There are a number of possible causes:

a) hostility against rejecting, controlling or seductive mothers.
b) weakened self-control as in men suffering from alcohol or drug abuse. It is difficult to prove cause and effect here.
c) sociopathic tendencies
d) an attempt to defend oneself from homosexual tendencies.

CHILD MOLESTERS

1. Paedophilia: this is the love of children with the expressed desire for immature sexual gratification with prepubertal children signifying
   – a maturational lag in adolescents
   – regression from adult sensuality caused by negative life experiences in the middle-aged offender
   – problems of loneliness in men aged 50–60
   – passive aggression where there has been a failure to establish significant relationships with the opposite sex for a man in his 20s.
2. Exhibitionists
   Indecent exposure

The legal implications of these offences vary from country to country. It may be regarded as an act of aggression or as a sexual act and this has attendant problems.

Our time has come to:

1. Be thoroughly informed about child sexual abuse in general and specifically within our church communities.
2. Assess the needs of our church communities with regard to both prevention and therapy.
3. Educate ourselves and our Christian Education personnel (Sunday school teachers and youth workers) in the detection and counselling of children and women who have been sexually abused.
4. Work with local agencies to develop awareness of the problem within our own congregation and community.
5. Assess the counselling resources of our own churches and communities. Could they provide better services with better training? How can we arrange this?
6. Extend our concern to other areas of family/domestic violence.

The church can help.

The greatest need of the abused is for love, acceptance and affirmation. Lack of understanding and compassion within the church for the wounded and broken hearted needs to be redressed. The long-time male domination of the church has left the church crippled in ministering to women who have been hurt by men. Begin to listen, hear and encourage, comfort and journey with the abused or survivors of abuse through to their total healing.

Help them to accept their past as a fact by helping them to face it and talk about it. This will lead to catharsis.

Help them not to deny their anger but to deal with it constructively. Repressed anger only becomes misdirected with time.

Help them to choose to forgive.

- This is not just excusing the sin.
- It is bearing the pain of another's sin against you.
- It is the letting go of resentment and bitterness: emptying the heart of anger and hatred and receiving God's love and forgiveness.

There is a need for healing.

Do not expect instant miracles. As with physical injuries healing sometimes takes time.

Determination to get well has to be present. The mind can be renewed by the Scriptures. 'He sent his word and healed them and delivered them from destruction' (Ps. 107:20).

Prayer is an essential part of the healing process.

Encourage self-forgiveness and self-acceptance.

Our time has come!

15

Christian Stewardship: Poverty and Hunger

INONGE MBIKUSITA-LEWANIKA

In discussing Christian stewardship, poverty and hunger we do well to examine the following words: steward, stewardship and Christian. We are all familiar with poverty and hunger. Some of us may have experienced poverty. Of course, we can be poor both materially and spiritually. Jesus Christ commended spiritual poverty in order to obtain spiritual fulfilment. In his earthly life he encountered many forms of physical poverty and wherever he met people in need he set them free from their needs.

At one time or another each of us has known hunger. But we may not be familiar with perpetual hunger. Some of God's children in our respective countries are usually hungry. There are children who are born into poverty and hunger. For these the world and life itself means hunger and poverty.

STEWARD

The Oxford dictionary defines a steward as 'someone entrusted with the management of another's property, especially the paid manager of a great house or estate'.

Dr. Han explains a steward as 'one who is entrusted with the property of someone else and disposes the same according to the wishes of the donor'.[1]

This definition is particularly useful to us as Christians. God has entrusted us with his property to dispense. He has also given us instructions about how to carry this out. In the first place God has entrusted us with life. He has also given us various gifts, such as possessions, time, abilities, families, influence, friends, money etc.[2]

The apostle Peter and Paul throw some light on what a steward should be.

Peter writes: 'As every man has received the gift, even so minister the same one to another as good stewards of the manifold grace of God' (1 Pet. 4:10).

According to Paul, 'It is required in stewards that a man (woman) be found faithful' (1 Cor. 4:2).

STEWARDSHIP

Dr. Han & Dr. Haggai define Christian stewardship in this way:

Christian stewardship is the practice of systematic and proportionate giving of time, material possessions, and all God's gifts to us in the conviction that these are a trust from God, to be used in His Service for the benefit of mankind in grateful acknowledgement of Christ's redeeming love.

The Lord Jesus himself summarized the instruction of the master/property owner to the steward as, 'Occupy till I come'. He took stewardship very seriously in the examples he gave in his teaching. We are to take our stewardship very seriously, intelligently and actively. He condemned harshly the steward who took the easy way out by burying the talent.

Dr. Haggai urges us:

Set your goals. Lay out your plans of action, make your commitment for fulfilling these goals, look to the Lord for grace and guidance and decisively move ahead.[3]

He urges us to turn deals into first class operations.

He who does the work is not so profitable as he who multiplies . . . turn a ministry of addition into a ministry of multiplication.[4]

J. F. MacArthur urges us to

Help change the world for good – influence lives, even millions of lives – penetrate anti-Christian areas with the message of Christ's redeeming sacrifice.[5]

Stewardship is not to be carried out haphazardly. Christians need to approach it as seriously as business men and women plan, carry out and evaluate their activities. We are called to invest intelligently and attain the maximum dividends in all areas of our stewardship. This involves the use of time, abilities, property etc.

CHRISTIAN

It is also necessary to review the word, 'Christian'. Some people think they become Christians by being born in a Christian country, or by having a Christian family, or by attending church, if only on special occasions. Some people think they are Christians because they were baptized as infants.

What then is a Christian? It is one who is Christ-like. The first time the term was used was in Antioch where the local people noticed the behaviour of the followers of Jesus and noted how like him they were in their conduct, their conversation and their way of life. So they were nicknamed 'Christians'. To be like Jesus Christ we must know him very well. So we have to have a personal relationship with him. We have to accept him as an example to follow, to read his word in the Bible, to spend time with him in prayer. To help us to know him effectively Jesus sent us his Holy Spirit as a teacher to tell us more about himself. The Holy Spirit also transforms us so that we become more like Jesus Christ.

MOTIVES FOR GOOD STEWARDSHIP

God has entrusted us with his property and possessions. He has promised
rewards to those who are good stewards. But as Christians our stewardship is
not only for those rewards but springs from love and gratitude. God made us
in his image to have fellowship with him. When the human race fell, God
made a plan of redemption. He gave his only Son to be the means by which
we could come back to him. What can we possibly render in return for such
love? We return love and gratitude through effective stewardship. Furthermore our appreciation compels us to be the best stewards that we can be.

STEWARDSHIP TO GOD

Who is the Proprietor?

The Bible tells us that God made the heavens and the earth and everything
that is in them. There is nothing in creation that was not made by God. In
Psalm 24 David wrote:

> The earth is the Lord's and the fulness thereof; the world and they that dwell
> therein. For he hath founded it upon the waters.

God owns everything in heaven and earth. As the prophet Haggai
reminded his people, 'The silver is mine and the gold is mine, declares the
Lord' (Hag. 2:8).

Not only these material things but we ourselves belong to God. We are his
people and the 'sheep of his pasture'. He gives us our capacity to think and
evaluate, our opportunities and many other things.

In his divine wisdom God entrusted his creation to man. In Psalm 8 the
psalmist ponders on the greatness of the universe and the smallness of man.
But he goes on to say:

> Thou madest him to have dominion over the works of thy hands. Thou hast put all
> things under his feet.

Not only has God done this, but he also entrusts to people the wealth of his
creation. In Deuteronomy 8:18 we are told:

> But you shall remember the Lord your God for it is he who is giving you power to
> make wealth.

God allows some of us to make money and multiply it. But in the process
some of us forget that the money and the wealth belong to God. G. W.
Rutland, a multi-millionaire disclaims personal credit for his wealth.

> You know, those of us to whom God has entrusted money have to be careful lest we
> think we had something to do with it.

Some of God's children like Abraham were very wealthy. We know that he
honoured God and acknowledged his ownership. He used his wealth to

worship and praise God. Jacob promised the tenth part of his possessions to God.

Today we still need to acknowledge, as Paul reminded the Corinthians (1 Cor. 4:7), that we received from him all that we have. One day we will have to give an account to God of how we used all those things which he has entrusted to us.

Will a man rob God?

Not to use or to misuse God's blessings is to rob him. We rob God when we waste the time he gives us, when we fail to use the opportunities he provides. We even waste other people's time and opportunities. Not to develop the talents God gives us is robbing him. A buried or neglected talent will die and that is robbing God.

We rob God when we withold from him what he has the right to receive. Malachi pointed out to God's people that in their witholding of their tithes they were robbing God.

We rob God when we use our wealth selfishly. The Lord wants us to give because in giving we receive. Selfishness impoverishes while liberality enriches. The wise man tells us in Proverbs:

> There is one who scatters, yet increases more, and there is one who witholds more than is right but it leads to poverty. The liberal soul shall be made fat and he that watereth shall be watered himself (Prov. 11:24–25).

The Lord knows that giving is an investment and so he commands us to give. But in the present world we are under great pressure to give to all sorts of causes. Sometimes we have given foolishly or to the wrong causes. While the world makes so many demands on our giving it is not a very popular subject in Christian circles. Most congregations don't want to hear sermons on giving so pastors do not discuss the subject. Despite this, giving is essential because it is commanded by the Lord.

Paul encouraged the congregations he led to give:

> I have shewed you all things . . . support the weak and . . . remember the words of the Lord Jesus, how he said, 'It is more blessed to give than to receive'.

The Lord also wants us to give cheerfully.

> Every man according as he purposeth in his heart, so let him give not grudgingly or of necessity for God loveth a cheerful giver (2 Cor. 9:7).

If giving is an investment and so fruitful, why don't more people give? Many of us are still baby Christians. We are still egocentric. We are selfish and greedy. We don't see beyond the present moment. Our immaturity prevents us from acknowledging giving as a command from God. Neither do we see the great blessings that come from giving.

Giving is not as easy as it appears. In giving we die to selfishness. In giving we put others first. Giving involves parting with something. Those who give what they don't need, or what is old and ragged are getting rid of rubbish and not giving. Real giving involves sacrifice. However, this sacrifice yields much dividends. Again we take an illustration from earthly farming which Jesus gave us.

> Except a corn of wheat fall into the ground and die, it abideth alone but if it die it bringeth forth much fruit (Jn. 12:24).

Jesus also pointed out the folly of seeming gain which meant permanent loss.

> He that loveth his life shall lose it and he that hateth his life in this world shall keep it unto eternal life (Jn. 12:25).
> What is a man profited if he shall gain the whole world and lose his own soul? (Matt. 16:26).

Abraham reached a point in his life where he was ready to withold nothing, not even his only son who was the long-promised one! That is giving, sacrificially and where it hurts. Yet Abraham did not call this giving of his son a sacrifice, he called it worship. How we need to learn from Abraham about giving to God. In such giving and losing Abraham was himself given blessing upon blessing. The Lord continues to give to Abraham through his descendants, the new Israel.

Another example of a man who understood what giving to God was was David. When he was young he gave his praises to God. In later life he refused to give what had cost him nothing.

> I will surely buy it of thee at a price. Neither will I offer burnt offerings unto the Lord my God of that which doth cost me nothing. So David bought the threshing floor for fifty shekels of silver . . . So the Lord entreated for the land and the plague was stayed from Israel (2 Sam. 24:24–25).

Jesus, our supreme example shows what giving is all about. He continually gave himself for others. He gave his love, his time, his powers, his glory, until at the end he gave his very life. For our sakes he left his throne of glory. For us he became poor so that we may become rich children of God and joint heirs with Jesus.

Giving Intelligently

To rob God and not to give is foolishness. An example is given in the Bible of a foolish rich man who kept all his harvest for himself. He thought he would live to enjoy it but he suddenly lost it all. The Lord Jesus condemned this man. 'Thou fool, this night thy soul shall be required of thee. Then whose shall those things be which thou hast provided? So is he that layeth up treasure for himself and is not rich towards God (Lk. 12:20–21).

There can also be misuse in giving. MacArthur makes the folllowing observation:

> We see both exploitation and neglect. On the one hand Christians are being robbed blind through high-pressure advertising. On the other, some believers are robbing God because they have no understanding of what God expects of their giving.[6]

The Bible gives us examples of people who misused wealth and possessions to their own peril. Achan through theft brought defeat upon Israel. Ananias and Sapphira dealt dishonestly with their property. The result of their lie was instant death. Judas sold Jesus for thirty pieces of silver and lost his life and his soul. Solomon, the great King, gave in to idolatry and degenerated from a great, wealthy, wise king into an abomination to the Lord.

Many people today disobey the command given to their own cost. It has been said that some people spend years making money but don't plan how to spend it. They spend it in minutes.

We need to give with God's guidance and intelligently. We need to check appeals and requests carefully. We need God's direction as to what to give and when and to whom. We may be called to give time, care, a listening ear, counsel, clothing, food, money etc.

Sometimes those who give money are choosing the easiest way out. It may take more time to investigate the need and what is required for the situation than to give money. A person may need more friendship and more love rather than more money.

Some people give to gain influence, votes, favours etc. Some give to show favouritism or in fear. Giving for selfish reasons is not investing in God, the owner of everything.

The Bible urges us to honour our vows, to pay our debts and not to owe anything except brotherly love.

How much should we give?

Our guidance to this is found in Proverbs. 'Honour the Lord with thy substance and with the first fruits of thine increase' (3:9–10).

MacArthur also gives us food for thought about giving.

> When you consider how much God has given you, can you possibly set a limit (e.g. 10%) on how much to give to Him? He has given spontaneously and totally, freewill giving at its absolute best. Dare you do less?[7]

But what matters in the question of giving is not really how much we give. It is the attitude in which we give. It is the parting with the gift and perhaps what remains afterwards.

Luke in his Gospel tells us how one day Jesus looked at rich men casting their gifts into the treasury. He also saw a poor widow who put in two mites. After seeing this Jesus taught us the truth about giving. 'Of a truth I say unto you, that this poor widow hath cast in more than they all' (Lk. 21:).

In many cases the church today does not see the widow's mite. The church notices only the rich and their offerings. Sometimes the rich are invited to sit on Boards, they are made deacons, accepted into church membership for what they will put in the offering. The church may even accept money earned by dubious means or grabbed from the poor just to fatten the church bank account.

So how can the widow's mite be worth more than the hundred and fifty dollar bills, shillings or kwacha? The Lord Jesus replies: 'For all these of their abundance cast in unto the offerings of God, but she of her penury (poverty) hath cast in all the living that she had' (21:4).

The widow gave all that she had. She had nothing left except her love for God and her dependence on him. Some of the rich were just getting rid of what they did not need. Some gave to be seen of men and to show off. Some gave to gain influence or popularity. Of course, the rich who gave all that they had truly gave. The Lord took note of their giving.

Thank God who knows our hearts and notices when we truly give.

A right attitude to money

One of the most misquoted verses in the Bible is in 1 Timothy 6:10.

> The love of money is the root of all evil which some, coveting after, have erred from the faith, and pierced themselves through with many sorrows.

The Bible does not say that money is evil or the root of evil. It says that love of money is the root of evil. Money makes a good servant but a terrible master. There are those who worship money. It becomes more important than God or human relationships or one's family. A person who substitutes money for God is doomed in this life as well as in the life to come.

God gives us money to use for his glory and service. Jesus said that we cannot serve two masters, God and mammon. But some people have suggested that we can serve God with mammon (money). We can use it to accomplish the purpose of God, to extend his kingdom, to win souls. Money as a servant can be used to God's glory.

Giving out of love

The Lord does not force us to give. On the other hand he has given us an excellent example of giving.

> For God so loved the world that he gave his only Son, that whosoever believeth in him should not perish but have everlasting life (Jn. 3:16).

God loves us so much that we can rely on the words Paul wrote: 'My God shall supply all your need according to his riches in glory' (Philp. 4:19).

We have already seen how the Lord Jesus ..imself demonstrated his love in the way in which he gave himself both in life and in death.

Where there is love, there is giving. Even in human relationships love expresses itself in sharing and giving. There is giving of love, self, time, energy etc. There is continuous giving.

Giving as worship

We have already seen this in the life of Abraham but we see it also in the action of Mary Magdalene. After Mary had come to know Jesus she was grateful and loved the Master dearly. Therefore she worshipped the Lord with the best that she had. Some of the disciples called this worship extravagence because they had other motives. Jesus rebuked them in the same way as he might rebuke those who would rather spend their money on dog food, cosmetics, excessive sport etc. at the expense of real needs. Jesus told them that they would always have the poor with them. They should continue to help them and to work for them. However, at that moment, the greatest priority lay in worshipping, loving and giving to Jesus. In the economics and timing of God the anointing with the oil was in preparation for the Lord's burial. God takes whatever we offer him and uses it to the maximum. We need not fear the Judas Iscariots of today. Let us give to God extravagently of our time, precious resources, abilities, talents and all that he has given us. If we love God, we will give. For where our treasure is, there will our hearts be.

Time

We need to view time as precious and valuable. We need to understand that God gives us time to manage it effectively as good stewards. Surely we shall have to give an account of how we wasted our time.

In many parts of Africa people take pride in 'African time'. This means keeping people waiting, doing things late etc. We need to get rid of this thinking, this sloppiness and laziness. True, pre-colonial Africa had no watches or clocks. However, the people had time which they utilized to accomplish tasks. There were planting seasons, times for weeding, harvesting etc. There were times for hunting and fishing. There were times for building and repairing houses. They had goals which they had accomplished within their own framework of time.

The last generation of Africans who went through mission schools certainly were time-conscious people. The old civil servants, preachers, teachers and health workers kept time. Many of us were brought up by parents who kept time and insisted that we too keep time.

Why then all this 'African time' business? This attitude needs to be confronted, rebuked and buried. If we waste our time and other people's then we are poor stewards of God's time. We need to receive time as a gift from God and use it effectively and efficiently. May God help us to value time, keep it and utilize it to the maximum for the glory of God and the extension of his kingdom.

STEWARDSHIP TO CAESAR

The Scribes and the Pharisees tried many times to trap Jesus by asking tricky questions. One day they asked him, 'Is it lawful to give tribute to Caesar or not?' (Mk. 12:14). In reply Jesus told them to bring him a penny. He then asked, 'Whose is this image and superscription?' The Scribes and the Pharisees acknowledged that the coins bore Caesar's image. The Lord gave them an answer which was true then and is true for us today. 'Render to Caesar the things that are Caesar's and to God the things that are God's' (Mk. 12:17).

The challenge for us today is to know clearly what belongs to God and what belongs to Caesar, the earthly rulers. A closer walk with God and the direction of his Holy Spirit will leave us in no doubt as to what belongs to God and what belongs to our earthly rulers.

One duty which the Bible makes it clear that we owe to earthly authorities is to pray for them. Paul wrote in his letter to Timothy.

I exhort therefore that first of all, supplications, prayers and intercessions and giving of thanks be made for all men: for kings and for all that are in authority that we may lead a quiet and peaceable life in all godliness and honesty.

Our prayers make a difference to the rulers and the nations. God is attentive to our prayers and responds. We don't pray enough for those in authority. Nations can be saved through prayer. Leaders can be saved and guided through prayer. Giving time for prayer for our rulers is part of our stewardship.

STEWARDSHIP TO OUR FELLOWMEN

The Lord Jesus said that we would always have the poor with us. God has a soft spot for the poor, the weak, the foreigners, strangers, orphans, widows etc. As James said, 'Hath not God chosen the poor of this world rich in faith and heirs of the kingdom which he hath promised to *them that love him*'? (Jam. 2:5).

There are many reasons for being poor. The Word of God condemns laziness. So those who are poor because they hate work or choose not to work have only themselves to blame. On the other hand, different circumstances can make people poor, large families, living beyond one's means, getting into debt, carefree spending etc. God has given us wisdom and intelligence which he expects us to use as good stewards. Surely we cannot blame God or anyone else if we become poor because of self-made causes.

People may become poor for various reasons: sickness, injury, death of the bread-winner, loss of employment or livelihood, political upheaval, refugee status.

Most of the poverty that plagues the word is due to greed and selfishness. There are plenty of resources to go round but some people have more than a hundred times more than they need while others have none. Some people hoard their resources to last a life-time even though their lives may not be that long. Some bury their resources in other places and countries while their brothers and sisters go hungry, unclothed, without shelter, water and basic services.

God cannot be blamed for poverty which is the result of man's greed and selfishness. He has set us as stewards over his creation and resources. He has given us laws and guidance to govern our stewardship. He has given us freedom of choice because he has not made us to be robots.

God is not pleased when the poor are mistreated, the weak taken advantage of. His Word tells us to give to the poor and to be sensitive to their needs. We are to have empathy and sympathy with them. The Word of God also says that we cannot possibly love God whom we have not seen if we don't love his people whom we do see. John challenges us that faith and works have to go hand in hand. He cites the example of someone who says to a hungry person: 'Go in peace and may God bless you.' What is called for is action to remove the need. We are called upon to feed the hungry, clothe the naked, help the poor, visit those who are in prison or sick. The Lord says that if we do this, even to the least, we are doing it to him. On the other hand, if we don't serve and minister to the poor, weak, needy, marginalized etc. we reject him and therefore cut ourselves off from him.

While the Lord met the physical needs of all those he came across he also offered them spiritual nourishment. He challenged the Samaritan woman at the well to ask for that spiritual water which completely satisfies the thirst.

As good stewards we should imitate Jesus. The quality of our stewardship reflects the level of our spiritual relationship with God. Therefore we should walk circumspectly, not as fools, redeeming the time.

Above all, we need to relate our stewardship to the kingdom of God. Seeking his kingdom is a first and urgent priority. It is also a command to harvest the unsaved into that kingdom before it is too late.

May God help us to be effective stewards.

NOTES

1. Haggai, J. E. *The Steward.*
2. Ibid. p. 9.
3. Haggai, J. E. *The Leading Edge* pp. 139, 152, 153.
4. Ibid.
5. MacArthur, J. F. *Giving: God's Way.*
6. MacArthur p. 16.
7. MacArthur p. 104.

16

Women in Society

RUTH-YANEKO ROMBA

I THE GENERAL ROLE OF THE WOMAN IN SOCIETY:

I would start by emphasizing that my aim is not to dwell unnecessarily on what we all know about, the woman's lot in day to day life, her struggles, her hopes etc. but rather, let us try to outline her active participation in building her country and in changing the modes which are 'imposed'.

(a) The woman's place in society

Africa is a large continent comprising large numbers of people with different traditions which are complementary and not disparate while others have such traditions as agriculture, fishing, the keeping of livestock, in common.

Generally in African society, the family is the nucleus of all social organization and we can certainly affirm that the woman is the central pillar around which society revolves.

It is therefore on her frail shoulders that the heavy burdens which determine the smooth running of the family rest. Waking up before everyone else, she is the last one to go to bed with several aches and pains, only to resume the next day. The woman is also the link between tribes, clans and the families where she helps to consolidate the friendship between two people through marriage.

In short dear delegates, all this emphasizes that no matter what society they belong to, women are struggling and even if their programme varies from region to region, we see that they are faced with the same problems. But in spite of all this, in society the woman assumes second place and plays a seemingly servile role.

We notice that the African man is accorded the role of 'public-relations officer', while the woman kills herself with her numerous tasks, and yet she is consulted more often than the man would admit. When he finds himself faced with an embarrassing problem, he always stops to think and it is during this period that he consults his 'pillow' in other words his wife.

Therefore in spite of the woman's intense work load, she enjoys a certain role in society and in some cases the husband who is conscious and responsible will treat her well according to circumstances, giving her the title 'mother of my children; woman; mother of humanity . . .'

(b) Current evolution of the woman's condition

We should note above all that the status of women is gradually improving since all governments are becoming conscious of the role that women can play in the process of development.

There will be no significant evolution in Africa without the evolution in the status of women. It is in solving the problem of women that we will solve our problems in Africa. African governments have undertaken the following:

– institutions have been created to coordinate integration programmes for women in development.
– women's organisations are growing up like mushrooms.
– during the last ten years, centres for education and training of women have been set up. In the villages there continues to be less noise from pounding sticks which have ceded their place to the roar of the grinding mill.

Removed from her studies for marriage, the woman tries all she can to resume her studies or to train on the job in order to improve her condition in life. But this is a slow evolution and may seem insignificant when compared to the gap which divides her from the opposite sex. In order to remedy the situation she has to make an even bigger personal effort.

If the woman in general, is at the centre of the community's social life, what about the Christian woman?

II THE CHRISTIAN WOMAN'S ROLE IN SOCIETY

As we have seen, women play an important role in society and this becomes even more important when we talk about Christian women. But before tackling this problem, let us see what a Christian is.

1 Peter 2:12 'Keep your behaviour excellent among the Gentiles, so that in the thing in which they slander you as evil-doers, they may on account of your good deeds, as they observe them, glorify God in the day of visitation.'

Dorcas did good works – Acts 9:36.

The Christian must help widows and orphans – Deuteronomy 26:12.

In James 1:27 we read. 'This is pure and undefiled religion in the sight of our God and Father, to visit orphans and widows in their distress and to keep oneself unstained by the world.'

Works alone are not enough for the Christian woman to influence her environment because giving out of arrogance is not giving. She must have love. Corinthians 13:3 tells us, 'And if I give all my possessions to feed the poor and if I deliver my body to be burned, but do not have *love*, it profits me nothing.' Several of us think that giving to charity alone is enough to obtain remission for our sins. In Paul's letter to the Ephesians 2:8–9 we read, 'For by grace you have been saved through faith; and that not of yourselves, it is the gift of God, not as a result of works, that no one should boast.'

The Christian woman must be the salt of the earth (Matt. 5:13). We must share our flavour with the world for without salt food has no taste.

She must carry the good news to her neighbours and her colleagues at work. Anna an elderly widow served God night and day (Lk. 2:36). Do not wait to become a widow in order to share the gospel with our sisters who are still in darkness.

She helps other women who are weaker in faith or who have marital problems, giving them the necessary advice to edify them. She must not be like Athaliah, daughter of Omri, who gave the wrong advice to her son Ahaziah king of Jerusalem when he was going to war.

She must serve others and not be served.

I prefer to let you discover by yourself all the social activities that the Christian woman could undertake in order to demonstrate her faith.

Is it possible for a Christian woman to play a role other than that which we have seen?

III THE RESPONSIBILITIES OF THE CHRISTIAN WOMAN IN THE SOCIAL, POLITICAL AND ECONOMIC LIFE OF HER COUNTRY

We are living in a consumer society where money accompanied by power is the master. As a result of this and of various problems, the woman is sometimes required to work outside the home.

According to her vocation and her capacities, she assumes functions which increase in importance. Her life is no longer reduced to being a procreator and the household servant, to wash the dishes and to be an object of pleasure to the man. The Christian woman should be a witness wherever she is.

The Larousse dictionary gives the following definition of a Christian, 'Lat Christinus – one who belongs to one of the religions emanating from the preaching of Christ.' In the Bible, we read in Acts 11:25, 'And he (Barnabas) left for Tarsus to look for Saul and when he had found him, he brought him to Antioch and it came about that for an entire year they were first called Christians in Antioch.' From this passage, we can deduce that the Christian is one who follows the preaching of Christ. It is in this category that we would like to place the Christian woman and the role she needs to play.

(a) The role of the woman in the family

Let us refer to Proverbs 31:10 which gives us a picture of the qualities that a Christian woman should have:

- she is a woman who runs her household with love and diligence.
- she reigns like a queen over her staff and her possessions. When we look at this book we see a perfect woman, an ideal woman of whom every man would dream.
- she is a woman of virtue which is a rare quality these days. This implies faithfulness in marriage and being available to do good. This virtue gives her a value which supercedes the value of pearls and we all know how valuable pearls are. The heart of her husband trusts her.

These days, the couples who hide things from each other are numerable. Each one prepares for the moment when . . . The woman more or less expects separation or divorce and lives in constant fear. This sometimes causes her to hide part of the family's possessions in order to prepare for eventualities. As for the man, he naturally does not have confidence in his wife; for him a woman is a woman! It is better for him to take precautions than to regret later on. A husband who has confidence in his wife can entrust her with everything, perhaps even with state secrets. She complements the man and it is only in this context that Genesis 2:24 finds its true meaning, 'For this reason, the man shall leave his father and mother and cleave to his wife and the two shall become one flesh.'

The passage in Proverbs on the woman also shows us the qualities of a diligent woman and one who is not lazy at all. She rises when it is still dark and gives food to her household. She plants vineyards, considers a field and buys it. In short, she carries out a lucrative business. She is an enterprising woman. In 1 Peter 3:16, the submission of the wife to the husband can cause him to change and to commit himself to the Lord. She teaches her children the ways of the Lord and she is her husband's adviser.

We can therefore conclude that in order for Christians to play their role in society, they have to start with the family, they must be good stewards.

(b) The role of the Christian woman in her environment

According to Proverbs 31:20 'she extends her hand to the poor and she stretches out her hands to the needy'.

She must be the light of the world. Matthew 5:16 'Let your light shine before men that you may see your good works and glorify your Father who is in heaven.'

She should be the salt of the earth and the light of the world as we have seen in Matthew 5.

(i) Examples of women who influenced their people in the history of the Hebrew people

The Bible gives us examples of women who played a great role in their time:

Deborah led the children of Israel through to victory (Jdg. 4). Ruth was blessed and she was able to preserve the name of her deceased husband.

Mordecai said to Esther 'Who knows if you did not attain royalty for a time such as this?' (Est. 4:13–14).

(ii) The Christian woman and politics

Should Christ's disciples be complacent, uninterested witnesses living in their ivory tower, oblivious of human suffering? Does not the Bible give us examples of women and men in politics? Joseph was Prime Minister in Egypt, Daniel was Minister of State in Babylon, David and Solomon were kings of Israel, the Ethiopian eunuch was Minister of Finance in the government of Queen Candace, of Ethiopia.

God therefore chose both men and women to solve the problems of the hour and to lead his people. It is the same today. The Christian with her head in heaven and her feet on earth should follow the example of the Lord Jesus who went from place to place doing good and healing the sick.

The Christian woman should be an apostle of peace and subscribe to non-violence. She should act peacably so as to encourage dialogue in her environment. Consequently the Christian woman should be a committed woman at all levels of the society in which she lives. She must commit herself to the struggle against evils such as prostitution, vagrancy, begging . . . against social injustices whatever they may be, she should fight against misery by creating small cooperatives and other groups, she should be available at all times and everywhere without sacrificing her family.

The Christian woman should be the mirror of society, she must be open. She does not need to worry about the future (Prov. 31:25). She should first seek the kingdom of heaven (Lk. 12:24–31). She should be an example to others. She should do her best by always committing herself to ways of justice and peace.

Today Christian women should not hesitate to take up positions at social economic and political levels to such an extent that they can fulfil their commitment to serve and not to be served.

The psalmist wrote: 'The earth is the Lord's and all it contains, the world and those who dwell in it' (Ps. 24:1–2).

Are we going to leave God's possessions to those who do not care about truth and justice? Each one of us must consider and decide.

IV PRACTICAL SUGGESTIONS FOR POST-PACWA

We should have more meetings of this kind in order to allow Christian women who hold responsibilities in their churches to exchange experiences.

We should create a solidarity fund to support social work initiated by the Church and Christian groups in aid of widows, orphans, outcasts and refugees living amongst us.

Part Four

Our Time Has Come:
Women in Ministry

17

The Cost for Women in Ministry

PHOEBE KIGIRA

1. QUALITY VERSUS QUANTITY (LUKE 14:25–33)

A large crowd was following Jesus. To many of us, this would be a sign of success. In such a position many of us would do our best to attract more people or at least to keep those already there. In the process we may at times be tempted to compromise the truth. Not so with Jesus. In the above passage and in Luke 9:57–62 and John 6:60–67, Jesus states clearly the demands of the Kingdom, urges his followers to count the cost and gives them the option to quit. Anything important is costly – it always calls for sacrifice and discipline. The Kingdom of God is very important – in fact it is the only thing that is important in the existence of man. It is therefore very costly. It is difficult to enter and it is difficult to continue in it (Matt. 7:13–14). When proclaiming the gospel, we need to be careful not to give seekers the impression that it is easy. That is not scriptural. Yes, salvation is free but it is not cheap. It cost God his life to purchase it. For us to enter into its fulness will cost us everything. Today as always, Christ is not looking for crowds. He is looking for those who mean business with him and are willing to pay any price because they appreciate the significance of the Kingdom (Matt. 13:44–46). Jesus is looking for quality disciples, not for sentimental crowds.

The Scriptures do not imply that the cost to women is in anyway special or greater than expected of their brothers. We should not allow Satan to develop in us a self-imposed martyr's attitude so that we look for problems and opposition where there are none. Then what is common to all God's servants (Jn. 15:18–21) will be viewed as special crosses for us. Men and women alike face difficulties and opposition in the ministry. John Wesley is but one of the men who faced problems from his spouse and from the church.

2. THE WORST ENEMY TO OUR SANCTIFICATION AND OUR EFFECTIVENESS IN THE MINISTRY IS SELF

(a) God's basic call and will for every believer is transformation into the likeness of Christ (1 Thess. 4:3; Rom. 8:29)

Christ is not looking for employees, but for a bride (Mk. 3:14–15). He wants us to be his and be like-minded with him. A wife can be an articulate homemaker but a painful companion to her husband because she is not one in spirit and purpose with him.

At conversion our sins are forgiven, the Holy Spirit takes up his abode in us but self is not annihilated. This explains why there is a continuous conflict of interest in our lives (Gal. 5:16–17).

The process of sanctification which starts at conversion and continues throughout our earthly pilgrimage is expected on the one hand to subdue and weaken self and on the other hand to develop christ-likeness in us so that we may be able to please God.

God is committed to change us so that we become like his Son in spirit and character. We are the temples of the Holy Spirit and so we must be perfected for that noble role (1 Cor. 6:19–20). If it took so much time to make the Convenant Box (Exod. 24:10–16) which carried the commandments of the Lord, how much more will it take to perfect us whose lives are the dwelling of God himself. At times the process of sanctification will involve painful experiences. This is normal and should be accepted as essential for our own good. Jesus underwent suffering (Heb. 5:8) and so do other saints (1 Pet. 5:8–10).

In order to be sanctified, we must co-operate with God – God will do his part but unless we do our part as well, there will be no progress (Philp. 2:12–13; Jn. 17:17). We shall need to develop and maintain effective communication with God through diligent study and obedience to the word and a consistent prayer life. For self to be subdued, we should consider and treat it as if it were dead (Gal. 2:20; 5:24).

In practical terms, it means that we ignore all that which emanates from self, its opinions and values, desires and interests, priorities and ambitions. We cease to seek any wisdom or counsel from it. Instead we adopt Christ's values and keep our focus on eternal not earthly things (Col. 3:1–3). Unless we become more and more likeminded with Christ, we cannot be of any service to him and the Kingdom (Amos 3:3). If we do not know the mind of Christ, we might be busy and wear ourselves out doing what we consider exciting but which may be of no value to the Kingdom.

(b) Practical ways of responding to difficult and trying situations in our lives and ministries

Appreciate that during this earthly pilgrimage, God is more interested in your holiness, without which you will not see him (Heb. 12:14). Ease of life and happiness are secondary. The abundant life, Jesus promises us in John 10:10, is not meant to be a life free of all struggles. An abundant life is an all-weather life.

Trust your shepherding to Christ. As the Sovereign Lord and the shepherd, the circumstances that he allows to come your way are the green pastures – that which are necessary for your maturing and productivity. Determine in your heart to grow and blossom where you are planted.

When a problem arises, with the help of the Holy Spirit and the word of God, search the hidden motives that are directing your actions or reactions. Are you seeking self-promotion or Christ's glory? If you discover that the motives are self-centred and self-seeking, repent and thank God for preventing you from persuing something that is not in his will.

If you are convinced that your motives are pure and that you are really in the will of God, accept your circumstances with praise and thanksgiving and a humble and teachable spirit (1 Thess. 5:16–19). Instead of focusing on the other people as the cause of the problem, focus on yourself and ask the Lord to change you. Act and react the way Christ would act. Have you been opposed and rejected by your own people? Have you been misunderstood by the saints? Have your rights been violated? Are you in financial difficulties? Jesus underwent all these situations and left us examples to follow (Jn. 1:11; Philp. 2:5–8; Lk. 9:57; Rom. 12:17–21; 1 Pet. 2:21, 23; 3:9;.

Be willing to carry your cross. Carrying the cross is not just submitting to the problem. It is being committed to do what you know to be the will of God though you have the option to do something else which is satisfying to self.

Do not compare your circumstances with someone elses (Jn. 21:18–22). Breaking of self requires different tools in different individuals. Ruth and Esther entered into the will of God through different doors.

Since we are being prepared for different roles, our training and circumstance will have to differ.

(c) To be a true disciple of Christ in order to bear fruit that will last (Jn. 15:7–8, 16)

You and I must be prepared to pay the price it takes. The demands which God makes on us are not arbitrary – they are those that are absolutely necessary for our being the kind of people that he can use for the specific work he has prepared for us (Eph. 2:10).

3. HOW CAN ONE BALANCE BETWEEN THE LORD'S WORK AND THE RESPONSIBILITIES OF A WIFE AND A MOTHER?

Differentiate between religious or church activities and the will of God. It is very easy to confuse the two. A close walk with the Lord and a sincere teaching of the motives behind our involvement will help us to know when we are in the will of God.

Where the will of God demands that you sacrifice the welfare of your family and yourself, then you should be ready to do so (Lk. 14:25–27; 9:59–62). We have the example of Hudson Taylor and other pioneering missionaries.

Give private devotion and prayer their significant place in your schedule. Follow the example of Martin Luther.

Plan and schedule your time and activities so that you avoid wastage. Make the time you spend with your family quality time.

18

Church-Based Women's Ministry

MARY LUKWAGO

INTRODUCTION

Women-based ministry has been quite central for several years now at our church, Nairobi Pentecostal Church. With a Sunday congregation of over 5,000 people, we are the biggest English speaking church in Nairobi and the whole of Kenya. About 60% of the congregation are women. Outreach to women and through women is therefore taken very seriously at our church.

About seven years ago, the ladies started a monthly outreach that was born out of a concern for families where only one spouse – usually the wife – was a believer. God tremendously used this ministry and it grew from house meetings of twenty souls to crowds of close to a thousand. Many women found Christ through this outreach and a number of homes experienced healing.

For the purposes of our discussion today, I want to share with you a model of a missionary outreach that has been central in our women's involvement.

MISSIONARY OUTREACH

Some of you may not know but in Kenya today there exist some pockets of the 20 million strong population, where the gospel has hardly been preached. Most of these areas are remote, difficult to reach due to unfriendly geographical features and weather patterns. It also follows that these areas are largely undeveloped and lacking in the usual basic infrastructures like communications, water and electricity. Due to the difficult climatic conditions these remote areas were avoided by the traditional Western missionaries.

Pentecostal Assemblies of God, Kenya, the denomination we are associated with, felt a need to reach these areas with the gospel. As a result a missions department was established with the purpose of training and sending Kenyan missionaries from other parts of the country to these areas. This has now been going on for about eight years. Support for these missionaries, many of whom have large families, has not been as readily forthcoming. They have to contend with a meagre salary of about US$ 10 a month. By any standards this is a very small amount of money for a family and we praise God for men and women that are willing to make this kind of a sacrifice.

Faced with these realities, our privileged urban ladies felt that 'our time has come' to be actively involved in supporting these families. As a result, the Women's Ministries or WM as the women's arm of the church is known, has, for the last six years, been heavily supplementing the support for these missionary families. This support is primarily in kind. That is, we provide them with household supplies – both perishable and non-perishable. We provide them with clothing, bedding and try to meet any specific needs as they arise.

In doing so our ladies have come to know the blessing of giving. In testimony after testimony we hear of how God has proved true his Word in Malachi 3:10 when he says:

. . . I will open up the windows of heaven for you and pour out a blessing so great you won't have room enough to take it in!

ORGANIZATION

In order to maximize on group dynamics, we have divided up into twelve groups. Each group has a leader and an assistant. Whereas we meet together as a body for worship, praise and edification, specific actions are taken at the group level. For example each group takes care of one missionary family. They get to know the needs and try to meet them within the group. The fellowship that develops at this level is also helpful for encouragement and spiritual exhortation among the members.

We meet once a month on Saturday mornings. Our monthly programme is varied but we try to minister to the soul, the body and the mind.

Let me take a moment to point out a weakness that we tend to suffer from as pentecostals or evangelicals in general. Our ministries tend to be lopsided in the direction of worshipping, praising, preaching and more preaching! While these are good and indeed should be encouraged, over-emphasis in these areas can lead to a double-sided kind of life where what we are at church has little to do with the life we live outside. Yet the Bible is quite clear that Christianity is a way of life. There is no better place to help women to cope with the whole of life than the church. If we as believers are going to be the salt and the light of the world, our faith must penetrate our homes, our spare times, our hobbies, our dealings with mothers-in-law, our community activities and wherever we may find ourselves.

At Nairobi Pentecostal Church WM we try to teach women skills that will make them better women around the house or kitchen. We also try to develop leadership and other qualities by giving various ones responsibilities within the ministry. In other words we are committed to developing and enriching the total woman.

A typical monthly meeting would be something like this. The ladies gather at nine o'clock in the morning, have a time of prayer together and then split up into the various groups. At the group level, the latest needs from the mission field are shared and people pledge what they would like to contribute. Some ladies offer to knit or sew, others to gather up requirements. For some it may be patching up some used clothing. This is also the time to put together whatever has been brought for eventual packaging and delivery. We also spend some time sharing personal needs and praying for each other.

After the groups, we have refreshments which would have been prepared by the group in charge of the day. This same group also organizes any special music and this year we have been doing short quizzes to encourage the ladies to learn the Word.

We then gather together for a final time of worship, praise and special teaching. The teaching varies from pure spiritual edification to everyday practical application of our faith. The morning is usually concluded with some corporate prayers for special requests, and the national missionaries.

It may sound as if we do a lot of praying. Perhaps we do, but we have found no source of real strength and power other than through prayer. If ever there was a time when the Scripture that says: '. . . our struggle is against the powers of this dark world and spiritual forces' became a reality, it is now. We need power to overcome rampant immorality, even within the church. We need power against the temptation of materialism, we need power against squabbles – which if your church is like mine, we are not short of. We need power to learn to submit! – many marriages are in trouble because women have rebelled against the biblical principle of submission. We need power and more power. Such can be achieved only through prayer. I do not think there can ever be enough prayer. No wonder St. Paul encourages us to pray without ceasing.

OTHER OUTREACH MINISTRIES

I have been talking about our missionary outreach. Let me just quickly mention some of the other outreach ministries that our WM is involved in.

We have a ministry to reach the single mothers and widows. Many girls find the Lord after they have had babies outside of wedlock. This puts some special pressures on them that need to be addressed specifically. We therefore hold special meetings for them on a regular basis. The objective is to have fellowship and encourage each other in the things of God.

Once a year we hold a ladies' prayer breakfast, a time of thanksgiving and outreach. The last one was attended by over 200 ladies and the event is becoming more popular. Our ladies prepare all the food. We try through this to reach our non-Christian friends.

We also have an annual dinner where husbands and friends are invited. At this dinner we also try to express our gratitude to the various paid and non-paid church workers.

We have been involved in outreaches to a children's home where we have encouraged the children in the things of God. We have also helped them materially by providing clothing and foodstuffs.

Our ladies are involved in ministering to the needy among us, the bereaved, the sick, the aged and new mothers. The women make time to visit the various members of the WM and the church at large. We try to pray with them, rejoice with them or encourage them as the case may be.

We also run a food bank. Like all cities Nairobi has its share of the unemployed and under-priviledged. Such people are coming through the church all the time looking for a helping hand. Rather than give them money, the church helps them with foodstuffs like beans, flour, rice, sugar and so on – contributed by our ladies.

Those are some of the ministries our ladies are involved in.

LESSONS

What are some of the things God has been teaching us?

1. I have already mentioned prayer. We can have fantastic goals and plans. We can be most organized. But if we do not have a strong prayer base, our efforts are in vain. At the executive level, we make it a point to spend time in prayer talking to God and listening to him.
2. By endeavouring to minister to the total woman we not only reach women but whole families. Let me give you my own example. All my adult years I have baked cakes and I am always acquiring new recipes. But for some reason I never took interest in cake decoration. So every time it was my son's birthday I would buy a nicely decorated cake. Two years ago I took part in one of our cake-decoration classes. As a result when he turned five, I made a cake and decorated it. What was interesting however was that by the end of the exercise, everyone was involved in this cake – his aunt, his cousins, his father so the cake became a rallying point for the family. It was a lot more meaningful to my son because he saw mummy prepare it.
3. By rallying around the national missionaries we have had a focal point around which we learn and benefit. For example some ladies have learnt knitting, making bed-spreads, sewing and so on in the process of preparing for the missionary families. The doing things together in groups has also drawn us closer to each other.
4. The church of God is full of talent and we must exploit it for the Kingdom. We have found that dividing into groups is one of the ways of discovering talent and putting it to use. Some are given to administration, some to prayer, some to ministry through music, some to teaching, others to exhortation and so on. Whereas at the mass level only a handful of people are drawn upon, each group provides an opportunity for the hidden talents to thrive.
5. I must mention also that over the years it has been humbling to learn how human we are. Women are known for their enthusiasm. That is the reason for PACWA. This is tremendous. However, it is also known that when we get together as women – yes Christian women – squabbles and power struggles and all kinds of disagreements spring up. I would be painting a wrong picture if I did not state that our church's WM has had its share of these. I have no desire to dwell on them here but let me encourage this meeting this morning to address itself to this issue. I have no doubt that divisions and disagreements are from the evil one. Yet they are so rampant in the church of Jesus Christ. If it is not within the local church, it is

between denominations. If it is not denominations, it is between tribes – and I am talking about believers – evangelical believers.

The question I leave with you is what shall we do to encourage genuine unity and fellowship among evangelical women and the church in Africa as a whole?

19

Hospital Ministry

M. THANDI

Hospital ministry is one of the most important – if not the most important – methods of evangelism for the following reasons:

1. More people pass through the hospitals of the world each year than through its churches. While in hospital, they are often in a condition of mind and heart to listen more readily to the gospel message, than when they are healthy, self assured, and prospering. Here they are conscious of their need of a Comforter and a Saviour.
2. The ministry of Jesus Christ was directed to the whole man: body, soul and spirit, and he commissioned his disciples to heal all manner of sickness and disease, to cast out demons and to preach the kingdom of God (Lk. 9:1–2). Jesus today still commissions his disciples to continue the same ministry – the Great Commission (Mk. 16:15–18).
3. Whereas churches are closed and public preaching silenced in countries where a tyrannizing ideology or religion dominates, hospitals remain open. Did you know human beings prize health as one of their most valuable possessions?

Because evangelism in the hospital is so significant and sensitive and can produce such a considerable harvest, it is important that it be carried out in an effective manner. It does not require great learning, but certainly great love and gentleness are essential. The problem of suffering has bewildered and distressed mankind throughout the ages. In hospital one is confronted with men and women who are not only face to face with this mystery, but who tangibly experience its discomfort. Remember that the shadow of death rests upon some of them, and that the hospital may be their last stop before eternity. According to the Bible they will spend this unending period either in heaven or in hell.

A large proportion of the three-and-a half years of our Lord Jesus' public ministry was devoted to the sick. He ministered compassionately to the whole man – body, soul and spirit – giving due attention to each dimension. He removed fear and loneliness, introduced personal care, met the people's deepest needs, restored hope and health. Jesus' ministry prepared people for life after death, and opened the way to all the good things God wants to share with us.

Jesus is the worlds' greatest authority on all matters concerning God and man; life after death, time and eternity, love and relationships. He commanded all mankind to follow him, to follow his example and his teaching. His approach is the best and most relevant today.

PRACTICAL PROPOSALS

The following are some practical recommendations on how to do ministry in the hospital. Go prayerfully and carefully. The people you are about to visit have been weakened by illness and pain. To a greater or lesser degree they are afraid and anxious. You are required to be both serious and yet cheerfully hopeful. Tenderness of spirit must characterize your bearing. Do not go till you have prayed earnestly, thoughtfully and compassionately. 'Blood and thunder, fire and brimstone' type of preaching is out of order on this occasion.

All healing institutions, whether they are large or small, have certain rules which govern them. Acquaint yourself with these and abide by them. Remember it is not a church or an evangelistic hall, but a place where the chief aim is to provide physical or mental healing. Those in control of hospitals are sometimes strongly opposed to evangelism being carried on in their institutions. Perhaps in the past they have had unfortunate and unpleasant experiences with unwise or over-zealous evangelists, or may even consider your visit as an unwelcome intrusion into the lives and treatment of those committed to their care. As a wise visitor however, you may become a valuable member of the healing team that surrounds the patient.

Your Pastor should obtain official medical permission from the hospital's matron/director for you to visit the wards. If a pass has been issued, this does not mean that you are at liberty to enter the hospital at any time without regard for those in authority; these include the security officer, the nurse, the nursing assistant, the doctor, the domestic staff etc.

Always ask for permission to see the patient if your visit is out of visiting hours; do not interrupt ward routine. Introduce yourself to the person in charge of the ward (station) and say you have permission from the director/manager/matron. Ask the person in charge if she/he knows of patients who do not have visitors and tell her whom you plan to visit. It is wise not to visit a patient during a doctor's round or soon after surgery.

BEDSIDE MINISTRY

Bedside ministry is different from mass evangelism. It is meeting the patient on a person to person basis. This can follow a ward service, tape ministry, or can be part of a planned witnessing session or it can take place while you are making a casual visit or working on the ward.

PRINCIPLES TO BE FOLLOWED

1. Having received permission from the person in charge of the ward, introduce yourself to the patient *by name NOT the church you are*

affiliated to. Ask the patient his/her name, and *show real interest* in the patient. This puts the conversation on a more personal level. Throughout your conversation continue to refer to the patient by name when speaking to him or praying for him.

2. Sit down while talking by the patient's bedside if a chair or stool is available. Sitting makes you appear unhurried even though you are going to spend only 5 – 10 minutes with them. If no seat is available, stand where the patient can see you without having to strain his neck. *Never sit on the patient's bed*.

3. Initiate the conversation with the patient which will lead up to the point of your visit. Trust the Lord to lead you. You can begin by asking casual questions: 'How are you?' 'How long have you been in hospital?' Always speak kindly and gently – never too loudly. Never argue to prove your point and avoid being preachy to the patient. *Arguing* and *preaching* cause people to build up defences. You may win the argument, but lose an opportunity to minister to that patient. Remember also that the patient has his rights to his own opinion even though it may differ from yours.

4. Observe things in his surroundings and relate it to spiritual things. For example if he is having a blood transfusion, you can tell him that this blood he is having is for the temporary relief of his condition, but that you know of someone who gave his blood for eternal relief. Observe the types of books on his locker, a Bible, a novel, ash tray and cigarettes or rosary and use it to make a spiritual reference.

5. Keep to the great and fundamental truths of salvation and speak about the person of Jesus Christ. Use 'Four steps to God/Four things God wants you to know'. Avoid the 'if you die' approach, rather speak of eternal life. Talk about fear, depression, anxiety and the Bible's answer to these.

6. Be a listener. Give the patient the opportunity to share his experiences. Help him to understand how God often allows physical illness to bring spiritual blessing. Be patient if he does not understand. Bear in mind that he probably has more than physical illness. Be respectful and do not say things that can upset the patient and cause undue emotional stress. Be prepared to leave if an emergency arises or the patient becomes upset.

7. The mind of the sick person is easily wearied and incapable of paying attention over a long period of time, therefore it is unwise to read an extended portion of scripture or offer too long a prayer. Also pray in a sensitive way when you pray for physical healing. Pray for the soul of the patient and include a request for divine blessing on all the treatment being given.

8. In the case of the seriously ill patient the visit should be even shorter and just a prayer may suffice. Even though the patient is unconscious, we can speak to them of God's love, his forgiveness and his power to heal. It is God's spirit which communicates with the spirit of the person. We can pray for the patient and trust God to do the rest. Medical science has proved that the unconscious patient can hear us; therefore never say anything negative in their presence.

9. While you are ministering to the patients, please bear in mind that the patient's charts are none of your business, neither should you discuss the other patients' condition with the patient. Keep confidences the patient

has shared with you in confidence. If something goes wrong while you are there such as a drip running through or if the patient is in physical distress, immediately draw it to the attention of the nurse. Do not give the patient anything to eat or drink even though they may ask for it, without first consulting with the nurse.

10. Be extremely sensitive to the patient's need. Listen with undivided attention to the things he says and those he does not say. Offer practical help, for example to deliver a message, make a phone call etc. Be available – leave a phone number or address. Make a future appointment to see him again – and be faithful in keeping it. The patient will eventually look forward to your coming.

11. Be prepared, after you have led a patient to Christ, to follow him up by encouragement, teaching and edification. Encourage Christian patients to keep on trusting the Lord and to seek for a deeper relationship with him. Spend much time in your private personal prayer for them, and ask the Lord to give you the right words 'in season for each particular patient'.

12. Last but not least – include the hospital staff in your ministry. Remember they spend most of their time with the patients. Some may be Christians; get to know them. They too can help the patient spiritually. Aim to make them your collaborators and an extension of your evangelism. In countries where hospital evangelism is not permitted seek to train the hospital staff in evangelism, prayer and discipleship.

THE TRACTS MINISTRY IN HOSPITAL

The distribution of tracts in hospital especially in waiting rooms has proved to be of inestimable value. Patients often have time to read – though a 'heavy' and congested piece of literature will put them right off. A careful selection of well written and attractively printed books or booklets will stimulate interest and will be of lasting value to a patient. *Discretion* should be used in *selection* and *distribution*, therefore a knowledge of the contents of the tract is essential. Have an idea of the type of ward you are visiting, and select the tracts in the right language which is best suited for the patients. Some tracts which are calculated to arouse, shock, awaken and thus bless an unbeliever when he is well, could prove to be detrimental when he is in hospital. The message conveyed should not scare the patients but bring refreshment, hope and comfort to the saved; advice, teaching and testimony to the unsaved. Ensure that tracts carry an address for contact purposes. The church stamp is most appropriate.

WARD SERVICES AND SINGING MINISTRY

Hospital evangelism may be done by singing groups from churches. (Keep the numbers low, say seven persons per group). When permission has been sought the programme could include a brief message, personal talks with the patients and the distribution of suitable books and booklets. Singing groups are especially welcome at Easter and Christmas time.

TAPE MINISTRY

This is one of the most effective tools when you don't have many people to work with. It is a fourfold ministry – singing, ward service, bedside ministry and follow-up. You need a suitable tape recorder, with good batteries or with a suitable plug outlet. You may ask your Pastor or a lay person to give devotional talks. Be prepared to follow-up, as many patients ask questions about the message afterwards.

FOLLOW-UP

When we minister to the sick in hospital we have a responsibility to that individual. We must continue to be available to show concern and understanding. Depending on the outcome of their sickness – some are left disabled for life e.g. paraplegics, stomiasis in which case practical Christianity is necessary, for example – washing, cooking, cleaning etc. Visit, telephone, write or invite them for a day or week-end and get to know their needs physically or spiritually and get to know their family. Encourage them to fellowship with Christians and make sure they have a Bible and some Christian literature. Don't become too familiar – refer the opposite sex to a responsible person of their sex.

ARGUMENTS AGAINST HOSPITAL EVANGELISM

Many and varied are the arguments given against hospital evangelism. Be encouraged though, that our Lord himself freely dispensed the gospel message while he healed the physical diseases of men and women. The paralyzed man who was let down through the open roof is a good example. Jesus first forgave his sins and then he healed his body. Hospital evangelism is sometimes opposed on the assumption:

1. That we are taking advantage of a person's weakness to constrain him to believe what he would not otherwise fully accept when sound in body and mind. The answer to this is that we are, in fact, bringing comfort and a message of hope, peace, and love which can only have a positive and healing effect. Salvation brings calm and immense joy.

   Also, we are commissioned to preach the gospel to every creature. God often uses a sick-bed to arrest a person's careless and headlong dash towards a Christless eternity. Many are in hospital due to sinful living. We need to look upon every patient as someone in whom God is expressing a particular interest. When sickness strikes, backsliders too are frequently brought to realize that they have strayed from the Lord.
2. That we make patients nervous when we speak to them about religion, since it gives them the impression they are about to die. In actual fact many people who are laid aside by sickness come under a severe and depressing sense of guilt, and are only too glad to be able to speak to someone who can help them find relief. 'I was brought low, and he helped me' said David (Ps. 116:6). In reality we are not bringing 'religion' to the

patients, but are telling them about Jesus Christ, whose kindness and help to the sick and suffering is acknowledged by Christians and non-Christians alike.

DISCUSSION QUESTIONS

1. Hospital Chaplains' Ministry – is it for men only?
2. How about the children in hospital?
3. Reaching the Health Field workers and relatives.

CONCLUSION AND SUMMARY

Do not look upon hospital ministry as of secondary value in your ministry. The New Testament records several instances of private and personal interviews the Lord Jesus and his apostles held with individuals. These meetings had important and far-reaching results, and are recounted for our encouragement and enlightenment. God's love for the sick is your guarantee that he will enable you to reach them.

20

Children's Evangelism

MARY N. LAR

WHO ARE THE CHILDREN?

Children are the young offspring of human beings. They are the products of a man and woman. They are deemed to be children when in their infancy i.e. from birth to about one year and after that they are still referred to as children until they are about the age of twelve, when they became teenagers or youths.

After twelve years, they gradually develop into adulthood.

There are certain characteristics associated with children which the adults involved in evangelizing them must know and take into consideration so that their approach to children will be effective and result-oriented. These characteristics are basic in all children. Their developmental process is in four distinct areas:

1. The Physical aspect
2. The Intellectual aspect
3. The Social aspect
4. The Emotional aspect

All the four form the total child. Here we can add to the intellectual growth, the most important aspect that links human beings with their Creator i.e. the spiritual aspect of life. The world does not add this as an aspect of growth. But Christians can not see the complete man without the aspect of his spiritual growth.

The co-ordination of these five aspects of growth in the children helps a healthy growth in the children. In Luke 2:52, we are told that Jesus grew both in body and wisdom, gaining favour with God and men. His emotions, social relationships, intellect and spirit must have been in a good state. The Bible also tells us that Jesus reasoned with adults. This shows a high state of intelligence. In Jesus, we see the full development of a human being and this is what child evangelism is aspiring to achieve by the power of Jesus for it is only he himself who can give it to them. The concern of child evangelism then is to develop the child in these areas.

It is important for adults working with children to understand the growth of children so that they work at their level and help them through their growth problems.

No one knows or can say at what age childen can receive the Lord. Children have been found to receive Jesus as early as five years old. One thing we know is that children are valuable in God's sight.

Their understanding is certainly not at the same level as that of the adults. What they can comprehend at various levels of development needs greater research.

How then can we effectively approach child evangelism? The instruction is to 'teach a child'; other translations read 'train'. These two words, 'teach' and 'train' form the foundation of child evangelism ministry which no Christian can afford to neglect. We can then approach child evangelism effectively from four angles:

1. The family
2. The local church
3. The para-churches
4. The schools

1. FAMILY EVANGELISM:

We all know that the family is an institution established by God (Gen. 2:24). Therefore a home should be strongly established in the Lord; it is only in this way that the family will be strong enough to give a good foundation for child evangelism. For it is not possible to have child evangelism in a home where there are disputes and unfaithfulness. Parents must first of all have a good relationship with God and with each other. This will provide a good foundation for a happy home where children can be loved, disciplined and instructed in the things of the Lord as we are told in Ephesians 6:4. Parents have the first responsibility for the growth of their children. This includes physical, mental, spiritual and social growth. Both parents should be involved in this task of evangelism. But in Africa we find that most Christian fathers keep a distance from the family. They feel it is a sign of greatness. They leave the mothers to battle it all alone. The duty of caring, loving and providing children with the right things for their total development is the responsibility of both parents. Some parents leave it to the churches, or the religious knowledge teachers in schools or even call on para-churches to teach their children. If parents depend on outside help, then they may soon discover that the devil has already sown bad seeds in their children. And you know once the children are allowed to pass the age of learning without being taught, it becomes difficult to do it later. Moreover children are given the first example of life from their parents. If parents shy away from giving this example then the children are not likely to take it seriously from others. The parents at least should take the initiative of showing their children a Christian example before others supplement their effort. It was as a result of a family's good example that a child who became an evangelist at the age of nine came to accept Jesus Christ at the age of six. William Carey at nine was already filled with the Holy

Spirit and was an effective preacher. His parents backed up their Christian example by taking William to Christian activities where he finally declared for the Lord. Many parents would take their children to Sunday School and drive them back home. Others would ask the drivers to take the children to Sunday School while they stay behind. This does not help children to take the church seriously. They will ask, 'If it is worth-while going to church then why won't my parents go?'

One family formed a family singing group with a boy of six and a half years as their leader. It was great, the Lord used this young family gospel singer to thrill the crowd and the family unitedly praise God for what he is doing for their family. In all the songs they sang, they portrayed the gospel. In this way the family were feeding the spirit of this child with the Word of God. Here the child became what the family is, in its true sense.

At that age, the child had testimonies to share, so let no family take their responsibilities lightly as we all know that the home is where children themselves receive their first sight of the world.

The mother's role is even more pronounced in influencing the child, because her influence on young children is stronger than that of the father. That is no excuse for fathers to relax.

In evangelizing children, we mothers must ask God to deliver us from tension. As we all know the task of bringing children up is not an easy one especially when there are many of them. A mother may wake up and find some crying, some getting at each other, some disobeying, some breaking things. This situation will no doubt build tension in the mother and naturally she may lose her temper. I usually find myself shouting and yelling at the children. The best thing that usually follows this is for me to cast my mind on Jesus. Then my peace is restored. You will agree with me if a child is to listen to any teaching about our Lord, he must be in a good state of mind, otherwise he will openly refuse whatever we want him to learn. No mother can do the work of evangelism where there is constant disagreement, yelling and shouting at each other. When parents spend time threatening their children or disciplining them, then evangelism will not be easy in the family. Some of us become too ambitious for our children. So we spend the whole day correcting them. The biblical concept of parenting is 'loving authority'. This sees children as individuals created in the image of God, and therefore we treat them with utmost respect. We realize children have many abilities and potentials, they are intelligent and have a moral nature. Consequently we relate to them with an awareness of all these strengths and possibilities in them. Yet the Bible made it clear that children are born with a sinful tendency. 'Evil men go wrong all their lives, they tell lies from the day they are born' (Ps. 58:3). This means they must be guided, corrected and disciplined. 'Correction and discipline are good for children' (Prov. 29:15). If a child has his own way, he will make his mother ashamed of him. As Christian parents we have the great task of evangelizing our children. We must overtly and covertly introduce them to Christ. We should discuss with our children the things that displease the Lord and give reasons for it using the Scriptures, so we ourselves must learn and know the Scriptures for this purpose.

We need the support of each other i.e. father and mother. But where a parent is single, the Lord knows why, and he has promised he will never leave us alone. 'Don't be afraid or discouraged for I, the Lord your God, am with you wherever you go' (Josh. 1:9b). The Lord is with us in the task of evangelizing our children.

We were told in Lausanne II in Manila that the churches in Russia survived because of home teaching. This should awaken all homes in Africa so they can respond positively to this very important task based in our homes. It forms the foundation of child evangelism ministry. It provides good ground for the seed which can be sown to great effect by the workers who form the local church.

2. THE LOCAL CHURCH:

Most churches are aware of their responsibilities to evangelize children in Africa. We see that churches organize Sunday School teaching for their children. Such collective teaching can be very effective depending on the teacher's ability to handle children as unique individuals with distinct needs whose greater need is to be led to Jesus Christ. I came to know the Lord Jesus Christ through Sunday School work, the missionaries took keen interest in this task and this gave me the desire to attend Sunday School. The teachings were meaningful to me because the presentation was at my level of understanding.

From my observation of the teachers who offer themselves for Sunday School teaching in Africa, nowadays most of them are not experienced in handling children. But the Lord has equipped and is using such teachers in this service. This the Holy Spirit can do. But at the same time the Holy Spirit has taught many how to handle children effectively, and this knowledge if shared will no doubt enhance the work of the local churches. Some of these points are as follows:

The teaching of children should be in line with their nature. God has made children to be different in many ways from adults and teachers should not be ignorant of this.

(i) Children learn best through play activities or games, therefore use this approach to capture their interest. Use activities for learning because they learn best by doing. This is the way God has made them. Activities such as music, drama, arts, use of flash cards, threading or stringing a verse can be used. This helps children to connect words of a Bible verse in the correct sequence. So they read it when it is finished. Balloons can be used; a word from a verse is written on a balloon; give balloons of different colours to the children with one word, get them to organize themselves in such a way that the verse will read fluently as it is written on the board or card. This game is like a jumble words game. Verses can be summarized to make learning easier. For example Galatian 6:10 can be learnt as 'Always be kind to everyone.' Flash cards can be used in the same way as the balloons, also jigsaw puzzles are useful games.

(ii) Teach children memory verses. They enjoy memory verses, the teacher can introduce rhythm into the reciting, to make the children interested. This helps the children to hide the Word of God in their hearts so that they will not sin against God (Ps. 119:11).

(iii) In telling Bible stories, remember to increase the length of time according to children's age. Younger children cannot sit still for a long time listening to one story, unless the teacher uses means of capturing interest. This lies in varying the voice, used concrete objects, pictures and occasionally asking them questions to ensure participation. Use simple language that it within the children's level of understanding. The use of symbolic language can confuse children. A young child will need further explanation.

This also applies to the teaching of songs and choruses, the words of which should be made clear because children's minds are not fully developed. For example, 'The BIBLE, yes, that is the book for me. I stand alone on the Word of God the BIBLE.' In this song, 'stand on the word of God' can be misunderstood by a child to mean stepping on the Bible. That is why it is important to explain all songs taught to children, especially when the words are abstract in nature. Children see things more clearly in the concrete form than in the abstract form. Sunday School teachers should lead them along this line.

We should remember that the younger the child the more helpless he is and the more self-centred. Each child needs to develop a sense of belonging and this is cultivated by showing him love. We have to develop in the children a positive attitude to the Bible. Let children hear stories full of love. Tell them stories about Jesus in a way that will appeal to their personalities. We have to pray the Lord to teach us as we teach children about him. A teacher taught young children Psalm 23 and a little girl said, 'I do not think I like God!' 'Why?' asked the teacher. 'Because God said he will make me lie down, and I do not want to lie on the ground.' This child is not ready for this portion of the Bible, so the teacher should work hard to explain to the children at their own level what some Bible words mean.

Sunday School teachers need to spend time in prayer, so that the Lord will give them the wisdom they need in teaching the children about his love for them and so that they will respond to him.

3. PARA-CHURCHES

These are organizations that have set their evangelistic ministries towards certain goals. Some of them have children as their objective. Such organizations as the Children Evangelism Ministry, the Navigators, the cadets, the explorers, etc, are all working towards the same goals. In Nigeria the Children Evangelism Ministry is making a commendable effort. This ministry went to the extent of building nursery schools and day care centres where they introduce Christ to the children. Some of the children are from non-Christian backgrounds and some have been led to Christ. They have trained a good number of Sunday School teachers and parents. Some of the teachers trained have set up Bible clubs for young children in their neighbourhood. This is to help children whose parents do not go to church or do not take their children to church.

We know that in some homes children are used to keep watch over the home while parents go to church. Sometimes the effort helps in bringing

Christian children together with others who attend different churches under the fellowship setting once a week. This also helps children to share ideas and principles for spiritual growth.

In their training they teach teachers some principles of how they can make their lessons interesting by the use of the following:

Gospel glove
Gospel umbrella
Gospel cap

All in five basic colours, white, black, red, yellow, green. All that the children of God are doing is to introduce Christ to the children and to help those who have given their lives to Christ to grow old and mature in him.

How can we lead children to Christ? There are various ways as the Holy Spirit teaches individuals.

Here are some of the basic ways as suggested by the Great Commission movement. This is summarized below:

1. Tell a child the Bible says in John 3:16 that God loves you.
2. You have sinned (Rom. 3:23). You have done wrong things by telling a lie, cheating in a test or stealing mummy's sugar etc. Sin keeps you from being God's friend and will lead you to trouble in your life. 'For the wages of sin is death . . .' (Rom. 6:23). God does not want you to ruin your life with sin. And none of us is good enough to go to heaven without God's help.
3. God provided his Son Jesus Christ. His Son Jesus Christ is the only perfect man. So God sacrificed him to die in your place so he can cleanse you from all your sins and make you good enough to go into his Kingdom. Are you happy? Then thank Jesus if you believe this.
4. Ask God to forgive you all your wrongs.
5. You are now God's child because you have accepted what Jesus did for you.
6. Now you have to live as God's child by obeying him in your life. Go to Sunday School always and read your Bible daily. God will bless you.

This simple approach done prayerfully will appeal to young souls. This does not mean that Bible stories do not appeal to children. First you start with teaching the stories and memory verses where possible before finally leading them in the way suggested above.

4. THE SCHOOL:

The schools have provided a wonderful opportunity for Christian teachers to evangelize the children. After all they stay with the children for more than half of the day. Christian teachers in schools should count it a privilege to be working with children. Such teachers are placed in schools to fulfil the Great Commission for children that is, to teach and train them for the Lord.

Many teachers in restricted areas regions, states or countries are happy to teach Bible knowledge in a roundabout way, since they fear that the authorities will not be pleased when they see them teaching it directly.

Christian teachers have ample opportunities to bring up children to know Jesus Christ but some of them use flimsy excuses not to do so. If only they will remember that our Lord will ask them to give account for their work with these children. Then they will take this wonderful opportunity seriously. The school provides a more stable opportunity. There is nothing wrong in teaching Bible stories.

21

Literacy and Evangelism I

DR. MAE ALICE REGGY

A middle-aged Turkana woman walked into a post office at Isiolo. She was carrying a baby on her back. In her hand was a small note. A close relative had died and so she wanted to post the note to her husband who worked in the distant town of Eldoret to inform him of the death. She had walked a long distance from her village to the town of Isiolo. She could not read or write. So she had found someone to write the note for her. When she reached the town, she could not find the post office at first, but a stranger directed her. You must remember that signs mean almost nothing to a person who cannot read. Once inside the post office, it took some time for the man at the counter to grasp where the letter was to be posted because the woman could not even pronounce the word *Eldoret*. After establishing where the letter was to be posted, another problem developed – how to get the details about the addressee. The woman spoke only her mother tongue – Turkana; no Swahili or English. To make matters worse, the postal clerk did not understand Turkana. With tears rolling down her face, the woman said that the relative had died and she wanted to send a letter to Eldoret to inform her husband, but she could not make the postal clerk understand her husband's name or address. Finally the woman was turned away by the postal clerk who shouted at her rudely, *Tafuta Mturkana ingine ambayo anajua Kiswahili* (Look for another Turkana who speaks Swahili) What a tragic story: the woman's husband will come back one day to find that his relative is dead – and buried!

This is a true incident that was reported in the *Daily Nation* on 19th July 1989. The article posed a question: who is to blame for the plight of this illiterate woman? Is it her husband? If he is literate, he should have made prior arrangements for how he could be contacted during emergencies. So he partly shares the blame. Is it the post office? Although they have expanded and simplified their services, they certainly should have employed someone at the Isiolo post office who speaks the local dialect. Is it the local chief? In many cases, they have not done all within their power to persuade illiterates to join adult literacy classes. I would like to suggest this afternoon that the church also has to share some part of the blame for the plight of our non-literate sisters and brothers because we have not cared enough to minister to the illiterates who constitute 98 per cent of the adult population in the Third World.

THE NEED

In 1985, there were an estimated 889 million adult (age 15+) illiterates in the world, more than a quarter (27.7 per cent) of the adult population. There were also more than 100 million children of primary school age (6 to 11 years) who were not enrolled in school. These children are in danger of becoming the adult illiterates of the twenty-first century, unless prompt action is taken. The majority of adult illiterates are women, the illiteracy rate being 34.9 per cent for women as compared to 20.5 per cent for men. In the developing countries where nearly 98 per cent of the world's illiterates live, the differential between illiteracy rates for women and men is 21 percentage points: an estimated 48.9 per cent of the women are illiterate as compared to 27.9 per cent of the men. The highest rate of illiteracy is in Africa, although Asia alone counts 666 million illiterates, three-quarters of the world total, Latin America has 17 per cent and the so-called developed countries are also affected by a related problem: functional illiteracy.

About 65 per cent of Africa's current population of 520 million are illiterate. In addition to low literacy rates, Africa has 1730 language (3000 ethnolinguistic groups) – about one-third of all the languages in the world. Today there are complete Bibles in more than 100 of these languages, New Testaments in over 150 and scripture portions in more than 300. Africa has the greatest need of Bible translation (more than 1000 languages) of any region in the world with the possible exception of India. Along with the need for the Bible, is the great need to teach people to read and understand the Bible. In Kenya alone there are over four million illiterates being 30.4 per cent men as compared to 50.8 per cent women. Around 31 per cent of children under the age of 15 are not enrolled in school: 27 per cent boys compared to 37 per cent girls. While non-literacy rates are dropping, with the increasing population the number of adult illiterates will actually rise by the year 2000 unless prompt action is taken. Although most illiterate live in the rural areas, still 30 per cent of the population of Nairobi have not gone to school. While nearly one-third of the city's population are non-literates, only 6 per cent of those in the churches have had no education. Clearly, the churches in the city are not being very successful in reaching the majority of illiterates with the gospel.

OUR MINISTRY

Literacy and Evangelism Fellowship of Kenya (L&E) was started in 1978 as a Kenyan faith ministry which is inter-church and inter-mission supported by concerned churches and individuals. Our primary aim is to help people to learn to read so that they can read the Bible with understanding. For example, the full Maasai Bible will be printed around the middle of 1990. However, illiteracy is about 90 per cent among the Maasai. So the printed text will be usable for only about 10 per cent of the population – that is, those who can read.

We believe that every born-again believer is called to bring good tidings to the poor, to bind up the broken hearted, to set at liberty the captives, to open the prison for those bound that the Lord may be glorified. We believe that adults who cannot read the Bible, a sign or a label on a medicine bottle are captives. They are prevented from becoming what God has ordained them to become. By teaching them to read, we are breaking the bonds and liberating them. Is not this the salt – the light?

L&E seeks to serve those adults, and their families, who cannot read and write:

1. We assist missions and churches (in any language area) to set up their own adult literacy programmes.
2. We develop adult literacy primers with Bible content using linguistic techniques. So far, primers have been printed in Maasai, Swahili, Turkana, Pokot, Kuria and Kamba.
3. We assist in printing newly-developed primers in cooperation with churches and missions. At present, draft primers are available in Luo, Samburu, Kikuyu and other Kenya languages in mimeograph form.
4. As a service to churches and missions, we train Christians through literacy workshops in how to teach both believers and non-believers to read and write. L&E has conducted literacy workshops in all parts of Kenya and in Tanzania and Uganda. Such workshops are implemented upon request from the churches and missions. During the sessions, Christians are trained in some of the following subjects:

   Understanding the Adult Learner
   Overview of a Complete Literacy Progamme
   Planning & Organizing a Literacy Programme
   Reaching the Unreached Through Literacy
   Literacy & Development
   Adult Education in Kenya & NGOs
   Pre-reading & Teaching
   Seven Teaching Steps
   Lesson Planning etc. etc.

5. We encourage literacy teachers to witness to their non-christian friends while helping them to learn to read and write. Most literacy classes meet 4 or 5 times a week. Because L&E teachers are born-again Christians with a burden for non-literates, each class provides an opportunity to enter homes and lives that otherwise might not be open to the church. Literacy provides a nurturing climate for adults who become Christians through this ministry. Discipling and spiritual growth are encouraged through follow-up activities.
6. Where possible, we assist in providing simple companion booklets to the primers, for example, *Habari Njema* (Good News) series published by the Bible Society of Kenya. One of L&E's future goals is to prepare simple companion booklets to the primers on topics such as health, agriculture and family life so that people will be able to practise their newly-acquired

reading skills and improve in all aspects of their lives. It is estimated that about one-half of those in Kenya with primary education will slip back into illiteracy due to lack of reading opportunities.

7. Where possible, we also refer adults and their families, to appropriate organizations for any other help they may require. For example, if adult learners need special reading glasses, we refer them to Sight by Wings.

L&E is one of the few Christian organizations in Kenya that deals with literacy. Part of our uniqueness is that we have already been able to adjust our teaching to fit the cultural context of the people. The adult learner is already painfully aware of his/her own failure and shortcomings. Mr. Josiah ole Kirisuah, Director of L&E has tried to build confidence in each adult learner by convincing them that they have already mastered some of the necessary pre-reading skills within their own cultural context. For example, every Maasai clan has a special branding mark. So there are as many cattle brands as there are clans in Maasai. As a result, any Maasai can see a cow and identify the owner because of the branding marks. In fact, there are more branding marks than letters in the Roman alphabet. Josiah ole Kirisuah tells them that letters are just symbols with names to be read. If they can look at the cattle brands and read the names of the clans, then they can learn to look at the letters on a printed page and read what they stand for.

Cattle Brands
> < V T X Y + =

Some adult learners think that reading is magic or that it is skill that only children can master. Mr. ole Kirisuah reminds them that a Maasai man can identify a particular animal – lion, cheetah, leopard by looking at the tracks: if hind or front leg and if the animal was running or walking etc. By looking at beads, a Maasai woman can identify the particular location from which a person comes. By looking at a leaf, any Maasai can identify the particular tree from which the leaf came. By looking at the shadows, he or she can tell the time of day. If they can do all this, they can learn to read.

In teaching reading, L&E uses the *analytic and synthetic method* – that is, in each lesson the most common syllables are taught through two key words which are learnt in contrast with each other. The syllables are pulled out from the key words and recombined with other syllables to form a *story* to be read by the pupils at the end of each lesson. In Lesson 1, the *story* will be a simple phrase or a sentence. Example: the two key words are *mama* (mother) and *makaa* (charcoal). At the end of the first lesson, the pupils will be able to read the simple sentence:

mama ana makaa.

(mother has charcoal.)

The basic principles or steps involved in teaching each lesson are the same:

1. Teaching picture words.
2. Finding picture words.

3. Teaching from the boxes & words at the bottom of each page.
4. Building words and using flash cards.
5. Teaching reading the story or sentences.
6. Reading the Bible.
7. Teaching writing.

LESSON 1

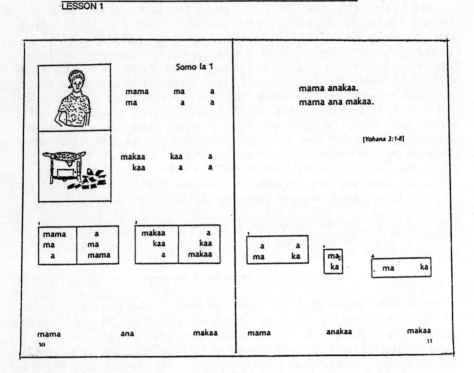

At the end of each lesson, the literacy teacher will read a scripture verse and explain. As they go further into the primer, passages are related to the lessons. For example, in Lesson 15, the pupils learn the word *maziwa* (milk) and then read a simple, but thought-provoking sentence from 1 Peter 2:2: *neno la yesu ni kama maziwa* (God's word is like milk). In Lesson 20, they learn the word *mti* (tree) and then read a story based on John 15:1–8.

Example: Lesson 20

Swahili:
yesu ni kama mti.
watu wa yesu ni kama matawi.
jamaa ya baba ni watu wa yesu.
jamaa yake ni matawi ya yesu.
yesu anataka matawi mengi.
je, wewe na jamaa yako ni matawi ya yesu?

English Translation:
Jesus is like a tree
The people of Jesus are like branches.
The family of my father are people of Jesus.
His family are branches of Jesus.
Jesus wants a lot of branches.
Are you and your family branches of Jesus?

RESULTS

Through our work in developing primers and conducting literacy workshops, we have seen:

1. People become Christians through the literacy classes.
2. Christians enabled to read the Bible for themselves.
3. Christians discover new ministries as literacy teachers.
4. Churches started out of literacy classes especially among the nomadic peoples in Northern Kenya e.g. Turkana and Boran.
5. Church membership increase among certain groups. For example, a church in Lodwar (Turkana) reportedly increased from 80 – 300 members in two years mainly as a result of literacy work.

Because L&E works among some of the smaller less evangelized nomadic groups, portable teaching kits have been developed. We make visual aids from pieces of cloth. We make *chalk boards* from dried animal skins and *chalk* from the paint used by traditional dancers. All of the materials are rolled up and carried from place to place. In Marsabit, the literacy teachers have pitched a tent and remained within the nomadic group until those interested have learnt to read.

OUR PROBLEMS

At present, we have a staff of two: a very capable and dedicated director, Mr. Josiah ole Kirisuah, and an office messenger, Mr. Patrick Malasi. Because L&E is understaffed, the follow-up activities are not fully carried out. The work of L&E is supervised by a very dedicated local committee on which I am currently serving as chairman.

Funding sources:
Donations from churches and individuals
Membership fees
Small grants from donor organizations (i.e. World Vision, Christian Aid Mission, Outreach International etc.)
Sale of books
Annual Conference fees

Because L&E depends mostly on donations from concerned churches and individuals we operate on a very limited budget of around 250,000 Kenya shillings (around US $12,000) per year. We consider it one of God's miracles that such a great work has been done for the Lord on such a small budget, but we need more prayer and financial support from the churches and the Christian community at large to help us minister to some of the neediest people in Africa.

22

Literacy and Evangelism II

LOIS SEMENYE

The importance of Literacy and Evangelism cannot be over emphasized. We heard about the work of Literacy and Evangelism in Kenya on Tuesday and the many good results that come out of it. For example some people coming to know the Lord, get to learn how to read and become teachers, relationships are developed and individuals develop spiritually as well as mentally. A new world for them is opened by their new ability to read the Bible and other resources. They have been given a very important tool. The blindfold has been removed from their eyes.

Can you imagine what you can miss if you do not know how to read and write? Unfortunately, many people live in that world of illiteracy. The good news is that each literate person can help to improve the situation. I hope this conference has motivated you and challenged you to do something in your own countries. I hope we will be able to come up with some specific applications that we can implement when we go to our various homes.

Conferences like this one can excite us and we get convicted. However, when we go to our various homes, the excitement eventually dies out. I am reminded that when I was young I enjoyed watching trains. They excited me a lot and especially if there was an old cardboard paper stuck on the rail road. What used to amuse me most was was the old cardboard paper. Whenever the train passed, the old cardboard paper would flap up and down very energetically until all the railway cars had passed. The old cardboard paper would then come to a standstill until the next train when the excitement would resume.

Conferences are like the train. They come and go. They excite us and challenge us. We get new ideas and visions. We are challenged and convicted to do something about it. However, when we get to our homes, the fire in us is extinguished. Soon there is no excitement, the conference is forgotten. The challenges and the convictions are seen again in another conference. This is the deadly pattern of conferences. PACWA and particularly we who are concerned with Literacy and Evangelism need not become old cardboard paper. We need to do something about it.

You may ask what you can do or give excuses that you are not qualified. However, I am assuring you that each one of you can do something.

First and formost you must be convinced of the importance of Literacy. Here are a few suggestions that can help you get start with a literacy programme.

1. Be convinced that literacy can be a very effective means of evangelism.
2. Share what you have learned with your fellowship, Church, different group, e.g. prayer meeting, Women's group, guild etc.
3. Include Literacy and Evangelism in your prayer calendar. Ask God for wisdom, people to help, financial support etc.
4. Get to know whether there are Literacy classes in your country. You can offer your help, facilities if needed or other things. The need for workers is always there. You can check whether there are literacy classes by consulting the relevant ministry in your country, e.g. ministry of Education etc., check with your country's church organizations, check in your directory various groups that would be involved with literacy, e.g. The Bible Society.
5. Make time for literacy classes.
6. Visit possible areas where there are illiterates, e.g. villages, markets, etc. Try to organize a meeting with them.
7. Educate others on the need for literacy.

There are obstacles to be overcome. The evil one is against evangelism and the spiritual growth of the people. Therefore, he will fight you at every angle. He will try to convince you that you:

1. are not qualified.
2. do not have enough money.
3. are too busy with no time for literacy classes.
4. cannot meet the needs of the world so why teach one or two to read?

This is a spiritual warfare. Our little efforts will be subjected to the devil's schemes. Do not gve up. We are more than conquerors in Christ. We need to focus on Christ and to be reminded of the importance of literacy and evangelism. Do not lose hope.

A friend of mine shared how literacy classes became a stepping stone to great evangelism in northern Kenya. Christianity was overlooked and regarded as an undesirable element in the society. The 'Christians' there were said to be oppressive, unfaithful, unjust, unkind etc. Islam was the religion of the people. Though the missionary faced opposition, she continued to be faithful, prayerful, patient, loyal to her call. She believed and was convinced literacy was essential for the people. Around that time in the early 80s Kenya was encouraging literacy. This was very helpful to the missionary. A few people went to her to learn. Her dedication made people become curious and want to find out why this woman was so special. Needless to say, a door for evangelism was opened. The obstacle was overcome. The literacy classes paved the way to other community development projects.

The advantages of literacy cannot be overemphasized: it provides a means whereby others get to know the Lord. People are given the ability to read from the Living Word for themselves. As a result they get encouraged in their Lord. People can read signs on the road; bus numbers can be understood. People can know what is happening by reading the local newspaper. People can read job advertisements or conference ads. People can communicate with others in writing or reading.

An illiterate person has been given a key to a world of reading materials by literacy classes. It is said that when you give a man a fish, it lasts for a single meal. When you teach him how to fish, you give him food for life.

It is not very difficult to start literacy classes. My church started one in the early 70s. The maids and the watchmen wanted to learn how to read. We were available and had a meeting place. Help was sought from experts in this field. Through the literacy classes, these people came to hear about the Lord, seed was planted in some and in some there was harvest. These people were also given a light to the world of books and particularly a key to read from the book of Living Hope.

You are encouraged to consult with Literacy and Evangelism Fellowships that are near you. If there are none, please feel free to write to L & F here in Kenya. They will be glad to work with you. They can assist you in training of personnel.

In conclusion you are reminded of the old cardboard stuck on the rail road. Do not wait until the next conference for your enthusiasm to be cultivated again, but go and do something. Encourage one another. Give hope to others. Give a key to the world of books by teaching others how to read.

Part Five

Appendices

Appendix I
PACWA Covenant

We, Christian women leaders from 36 African nations have gathered at Kenyatta International Conference Centre, in Nairobi, Kenya, August 5–12, 1989 for the Pan African Christian Women Assembly (PACWA) sponsored by the Association of Evangelicals of Africa and Madagascar (AEAM). We give glory to God for the great stride Christianity is making in our beloved continent. We salute those before us whose faith in Christ, love for humanity, and service to society has been both an example and a source of inspiration to us.

We recognise the enormous task that lies ahead of us. Our continent is afflicted by political instability, greed, poverty, hunger, tribalism, racism, structural violence, sexual discrimination and social injustices. Equally, the challenge of religious pluralism, increasing secularism and materialism calls us to reconsider our Lord's Great Commission and Command in terms of DISCIPLESHIP and not mere conversion.

We reaffirm our evangelical commitment to the authority of the Holy Scripture in obedience to the Lordship of Jesus Christ.

We stand at the thresh-hold of unprecedented and unparalleled opportunities. We strongly believe that 'Our Time Has Come' as Christian women leaders to:

1. stop the tide of ungodly liberalism and secularism with its resultant materialism.
2. assert the true dignity of women as found in Jesus Christ and contained in the Bible.
3. inject into African society biblical morals and values through women, who are the mothers of any society.
4. deliver Africa from moral decadence and ultimate collapse.
5. make disciples of African nations for Christ.

As PACWA women, we desire to affirm our oneness in Christ and our resolve, and to make public our covenant.

1. *Women in the Image of God*

   We affirm that God created men and women as equal bearers of his image (Gen. 1:26–27), accepts them equally in Jesus Christ (Gal. 3:28), and poured out his Holy Spirit upon all flesh, sons and daughters without discrimination (Joel 2:28–29; Acts 2:17–18). We reject therefore any teaching that makes women inferior to men. We equally reject any teaching that confuses a woman with a man; for while they are equal, they are not the same. As a human being the woman is neither less nor more than the man. Both are equal but distinct.

2. *Christian Character Formation*

   We affirm that God's purpose in redemption is conformity of every believer to the image of Jesus Christ, His Son. As a result we put emphasize on BEING rather than DOING. Discipleship is each believer becoming like Christ. There is no short-cut to this. Becoming like Christ will require the disciplines of personal Bible study; practice of the presence of God (prayer); fellowship in worship with other believers; sharing in love by word and deed with society; and keeping self from sin. In this regard we commit ourselves to becoming 'a woman of excellence' (Ruth 3:10–11; Prov. 31:10–31).

3. *Christian Home and Family*

   We affirm God's priority of godly home and family. The family unit is God's order for perpetuating the human race. God's blue-print for a Christian marriage is one man (husband) to one woman (wife) which rules out such practices such as polygamy, concubinage, lesbianism and homosexualism. Children within the family are a gift from the Lord (Ps. 127: 3–5), and they are to be loved and trained in the things of God. A childless marriage is as complete as the one blessed with children. As marriage is a gift from God so also is singleness. The Christian home should be a place for worship; training in righteousness; practice in love and hospitality; personal growth and social responsibility (2 Tim. 1:5–7; 1 Pet. 3:1–12).

   We are grieved by increasing numbers of broken homes in our society and the resulting agonies suffered especially by wives and children.

   We condemn wife-beating, sexual abuse, child abuse and any form of parental responsibility. We denounce the erosion of traditional family moral values often caused by modernization. We commit ourselves to upholding sound Biblical moral standards for home and family (Gen. 2:19–25; Mt. 19:11–15; Eph. 5:1–6:4).

4. *Women's Ministries*

   In the wisdom of God, the Holy Spirit distributes his gifts to women and men just as he determines (1 Cor. 12:11). We rejoice that God's power working through his chosen servants does not discriminate against women. Whether in the church or the society, and supremely in the home God continues to use women as 'shapers of destinies', for the hand that rocks the cradle also rules the world. African women have a legacy of industriousness. By God's grace, we commit ourselves to a restoration of biblical work ethics in Africa. We shall explore new patterns of ministries as we bear our witness in all sectors of society, church and home. Our way of operation is not competition with men but cooperation since the manifestation of the Spirit is given for the common good (1 Cor. 12:7).

5. *Evangelization and Discipleship*

To evangelize is to spread the good news in words and deeds that Jesus Christ died for our sins and was raised from the dead for our justification according to the Scriptures. To anyone who repents and believes this Gospel, Jesus offers forgiveness of sins, peace with God, victory over Satan and his demons, and the liberating power of the Holy Spirit to live a new life. Christ's Great Commission to the Church is not only to announce this good news but to make disciples of all those who believe, baptizing and teaching them to obey all that Christ commands. (Mt. 28:18–19; Ac. 2:32–39; Rom. 5:1–11; 10:9–13; 1 Cor. 15:3–4)

We praise God for the entrance of the gospel to our continent and thank those faithful missionaries. We rejoice at the growth of the Church in Africa. At the same time, we realize that there are still many peoples yet to be reached with the gospel.

We commit ourselves to the total evangelization of Africa. We shall intensify our efforts in such areas where women have proved to be more effective as in child evangelism, adult literacy and family evangelism while exploring new avenues.

6. *Social Justice and Economic Development*

We affirm that God is just and fair to all of his creatures made in his image. He requires justice, fairness, and good neighbourliness in all human relationships be it employer – employee; government – governed; leader – led; parents – children; husband – wife; citizen – alien; and friend – friend. Where God is biased, it is in favour of the oppressed, the widows, the orphans, the aliens and the poor, the majority of whom are women. We are appalled therefore that in many African nations women are discriminated against in matters of social justice; barred from highest levels of leadership both in church and society; and often denied access to economic sources of production. In all matters of social justice and economic development, we strongly advocate equal treatment of men and women. In fact, in cases where women have been denied equal opportunity, preferential treatment should be given to women.

Furthermore, as PACWA women, we are committed to improving the condition of women in such areas as education, health and income generation with a goal of self-reliance. We denounce all social habits that de-humanize and diminish the potentials of human kind including alcoholism, drug addiction and prostitution. (Deut. 10:17–19; Isa. 58:6–11; Mt. 7:12; Eph. 6:5–9; 1 Pet. 2:11–21)

7. *Ungodly Practices*

As Christian women, we affirm that God wants us to be holy in character, pure in conduct, righteous in deeds and altogether loving. While we stand in solidarity with the world (Africa in particular), we do not accept its worldliness which is a rebellion against God. Equally, we reject any wisdom of this world – religious and scientific – that sets itself in opposition or rivalry to God. Witchcraft, divination, spiritism, gnosticism and any form of occultism are rejected. Believing that greater is he who is in us than the one who is in the world (i.e. Satan), we shall yield ourselves wholly to God for an overcoming, victorious Christian life. (Deut. 12:2–4; Lev. 20:6–8; Col. 2:18–23)

CONCLUSION

For a continent as vast as Africa and for a task as challenging as charted above, we would need to pull together our diverse gifts, ministries and resources in order to accomplish our goals. We therefore commit ourselves to cooperation and a networking of activities. More than our resolve, we need to have faith in God and completely depend upon his promises: 'For it is not by might and by power, but by my Spirit' says the Lord (Zech. 4:6).

In the light of this we enter into a solemn covenant with God and with each other, to pray, to plan, to support each other and to work together until all of Africa is occupied for Christ. Grant us your favour Lord, energize us by your Spirit, and make us faithful for your glory! Amen.

PACWA COVENANT

WHEREAS I have read and understood the PACWA Covenant, and whereas I am in agreement with the spirit and purposes of PACWA, I hereby affix my signature this day . . . .
as a pledge of my commitment to the PACWA Covenant.

Signature: . . . .

Name in full: . . . .

Current Address: . . . .

. . . .

Church Affiliation: . . . .

_____

PACWA COVENANT

WHEREAS I have read and understood the PACWA Covenant, and whereas I am in agreement with the spirit and purposes of PACWA, I hereby affix my signature this day . . . .
as a pledge of my commitment to the PACWA Covenant.

Signature: . . . .

Name in full: . . . .

Current Address: . . . .

. . . .

Church Affiliation: . . . .

Appendix II
PACWA Resolutions

TO THE CHURCH:

1. We recommend that the churches establish pre-marital counselling to ensure that *all* couples are properly counselled and educated on *all* areas of married life. In addition to addressing the topic of family life from the pulpit, the churches should organise seminars, workshops, retreats etc. to deal with topics such as:

   (a) Husband and wife relationships
   (b) Biblical principles of marriages
   (c) Communications in the home
   (d) Sex in marriage
   (e) AIDS and other sexually transmitted diseases
   (f) Legal responsibilities such as will, joint ownership of property etc.
   (g) Management of finances
   (h) Training of children
   (i) Family Planning and Childlessness
   (j) Inlaws and extended family

2. We recommend that our churches take a firm stand against abuse of women and children and establish support systems for battered victims which will allow them to receive both spiritual and material help.

3. As Christians we believe that God's ideal for marriage is one man, one woman until death. Therefore, we recommend that our churches should take a stand against polygamy because it is against the teaching of the Bible.

4. As PACWA women, we condemn the practice of abortion and recommend that our churches provide adequate information on the evils and dangers of abortion.

5. In many of our countries, families are separated because of jobs, education, transfer and retirement. We recommend that such separations be discouraged by the church through family counselling and that the

Church and para-church organisations should set the example on such matters.

6. Whereas we recognize that many of the traditional ways of teaching children about sex are no longer viable, we recommend that our churches develop programmes for sex education. Where sex education is being taught in the schools, the churches should be aware of what is being taught and be certain that it is consistent with the biblical view of: chastity before marriage and fidelity in marriage.

7. We recommend that our churches condemn any force of witchcraft because it is an evil force and prepare its members for spiritual warfare.

8. The subject of AIDS should be given particular attention by the churches. Pastors and church leaders should be well informed regarding the transmission of AIDS. Christian moral values should be strongly affirmed and support systems developed for AIDS victims and their families.

9. The churches should encourage and support the education of women concerning their legal matters throughout the continent of Africa, both in the rural and urban setting and reinforce existing ministries which have as their objective to remedy social injustices.

10. Whereas about two-thirds of Africa's population are adult illiterates and the majority of adult illiterates in Africa (and the world as a whole) are women, we recommend that the churches be involved in establishing literacy program in rural and urban areas. Churches must see literacy as part of their comprehensive evangelism strategy.

11. Whereas the Lord has called us to be his co-workers using all his gifts, talents, abilities and opportunities that he has given us, we believe that the Church should identify, develop and use African Christian women, especially in evangelism.

12. We also strongly recommend that the single woman be recognised and accepted as an asset to the Church and her talents be fully utilised.

TO THE GOVERNMENT:

Whereas the governments in most African countries have taken some strides supporting the cause of women and children, a lot still needs to be done to improve the conditions for women and children and therefore we recommend that:

1. Our governments should promote and insure the physical, emotional, social, mental and spiritual well-being of women.

2. Because most women work about eighteen hours a day, we recommend that governments examine possibilities of examining the workload of rural women.

3. Our governments should provide child care facilities for working mothers.

4. In many of our countries, maternity leave does not allow adequate time for proper maternal care, and therefore, we recommend that maternity leave be at least three months, and time off from duty be given while a mother is breast-feeding.

5. Whereas in the majority of African countries, there is no inheritance law,

we recommend that governments enact a law protecting widows and children.

6. We recommend that our governments train women prisoners in different trades to assist in their rehabilitations in society.
7. Whereas the victims of the refugee problems are mostly women and children, we recommend that our governments pursue peaceful solutions to international conflicts so as to afford women and children to live peaceable lives.
8. We recommend that our governments ensure the survival, total development and well-being of all children and in particular provide educational and recreational facilities for pre-school children.
9. We recommend that our governments actively assist the abused and neglected children, street children and orphans by putting them into rehabilitations centres.
10. We also recommend that our governments pass comprehensive legislation to abolish child labour.

TO PACWA:

1. We recommend that PACWA develop on-going seminars and programmed materials which can be used in both rural and urban areas on topics related to home and family life. Such materials should teach young parents how to care for and train their children in the ways of God; also related to some of the critical problems that affect family life e.g. teenage pregnancies, abortion, AIDS, teenage suicides etc.
2. We recommend that PACWA assist in training of Christian workers to enable them to initiate and supervise programmes in their countries in order to serve and support the poor and marginalised peoples e.g. refugees, street children, orphans, abandoned children etc.
3. Whereas many women in Africa are ignorant of the law, we recommend that PACWA have a network of Christian lawyers to advise and prepare materials to assist women in legal matters.
4. We also recommend that PACWA research some of the African traditions (e.g. naming ceremonies etc) and develop a clear Biblical stand against any cultural practice or traditional that conflicts with the Word of God.
5. We recommend that PACWA develop an on-going resource centre for the purpose of co-ordinating ministries to women (i.e. networking).
6. We recommend that PACWA publish a quarterly newsletter.
7. We recommend that PACWA develop prayer ministries e.g. Day of Prayer, Intercessory Prayer Groups, Prayer Chains etc.

TO AEAM:

We express appreciation for your support and ask that all members be informed of the issues and resolutions from this PACWA. We also recommend that AEAM hold a similar conference for Christian men.

Mae Alice Reggy (Dr.)
CHAIRPERSON
RESOLUTIONS COMMITTEE